MW00800886

Dragon Age™

THOSE WHO SPEAK

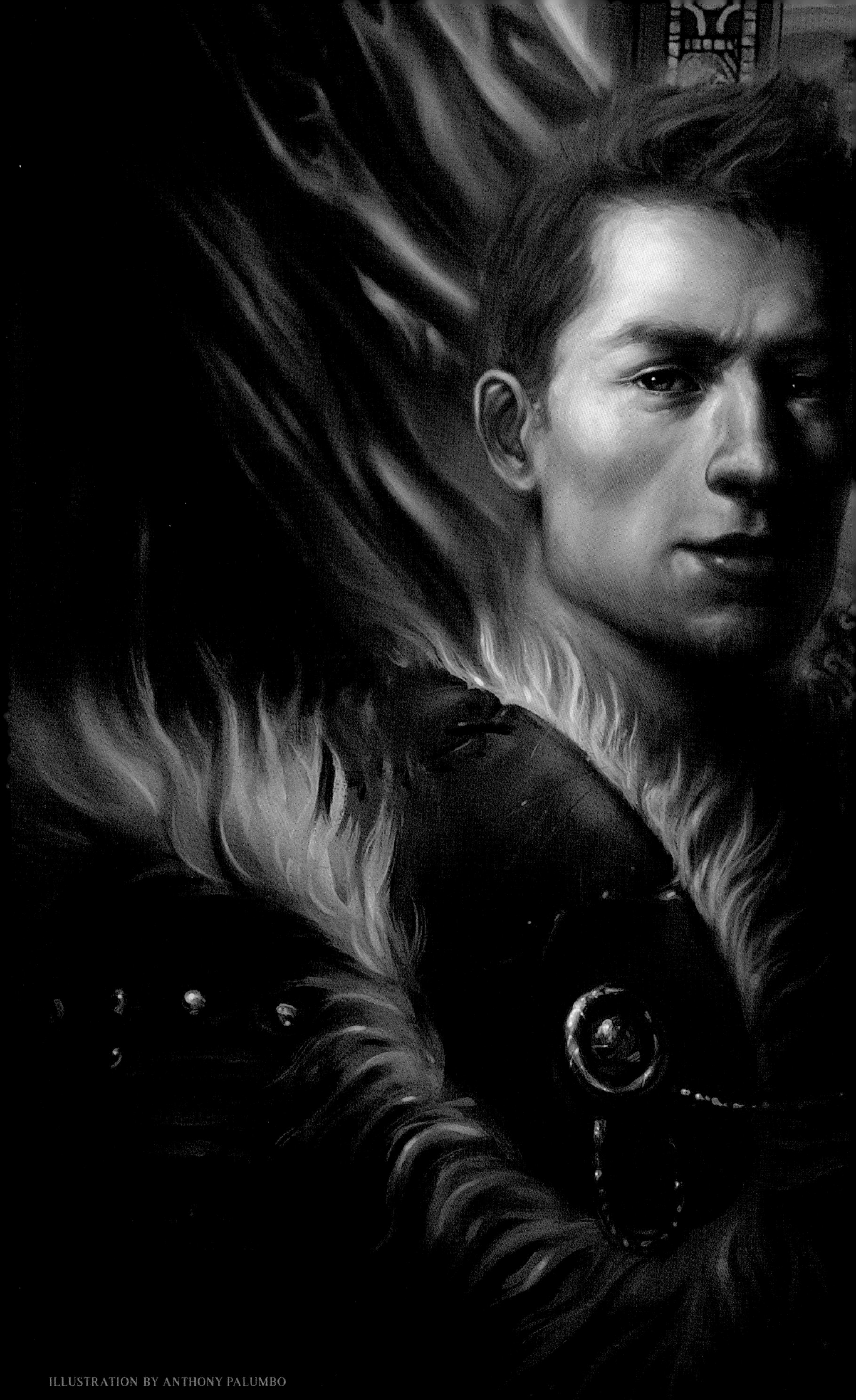

ILLUSTRATION BY ANTHONY PALUMBO

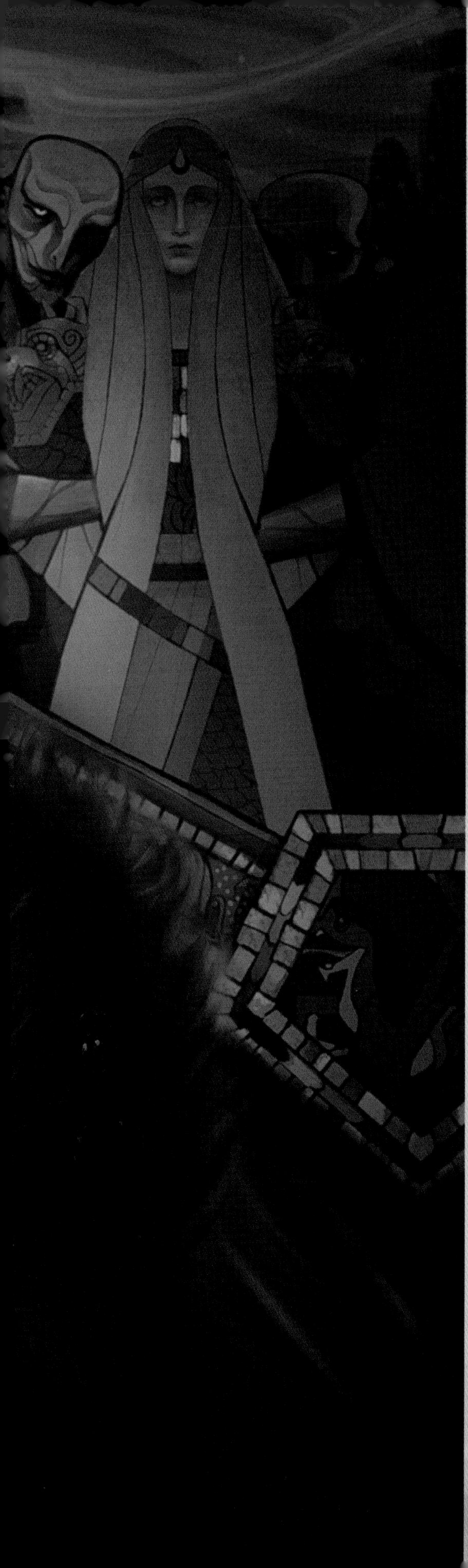

DRAGON AGE

THOSE WHO SPEAK

STORY
DAVID GAIDER

SCRIPT
ALEXANDER FREED

ART
CHAD HARDIN

COLORS
MICHAEL ATIYEH

LETTERING
MICHAEL HEISLER

FRONT COVER ART
ANTHONY PALUMBO

DARK HORSE BOOKS

EA

BIOWARE

PUBLISHER
MIKE RICHARDSON

COLLECTION DESIGNER
ADAM GRANO

ASSISTANT EDITORS
BRENDAN WRIGHT
and SHANTEL LaROCQUE

EDITOR
DAVE MARSHALL

SPECIAL THANKS TO BIOWARE, INCLUDING:
Matthew Goldman, Art Director • Mike Laidlaw, Lead Designer
Aaryn Flynn, Studio GM, BioWare Edmonton • Ray Muzyka and Greg Zeschuk, BioWare Co-Founders

---

DRAGON AGE VOLUME 2: THOSE WHO SPEAK

This volume collects issues one through three of the Dark Horse comic-book miniseries *Dragon Age: Those Who Speak.*

Published by
Dark Horse Books
A division of
Dark Horse Comics, Inc.
10956 SE Main Street
Milwaukie, OR 97222

DarkHorse.com
DragonAge.com

Library of Congress Cataloging-in-Publication Data

Gaider, David.
Dragon age : those who speak / story, David Gaider ; script, Alexander Freed ; art, Chad Hardin ; colors, Michael Atiyeh ; lettering, Michael Heisler ; front cover art, Anthony Palumbo. — 1st ed.
p. cm.
ISBN 978-1-61655-053-0
1. Graphic novels. I. Freed, Alexander. II. Hardin, Chad. III. Atiyeh, Michael. IV. Heisler, Michael. V. Palumbo, Anthony. VI. Title. VII. Title: Those who speak.
PN6727.G35D76 2012
741.5'973--dc23
2012025675

First edition: January 2013

3 5 7 9 10 8 6 4 2
Printed In China

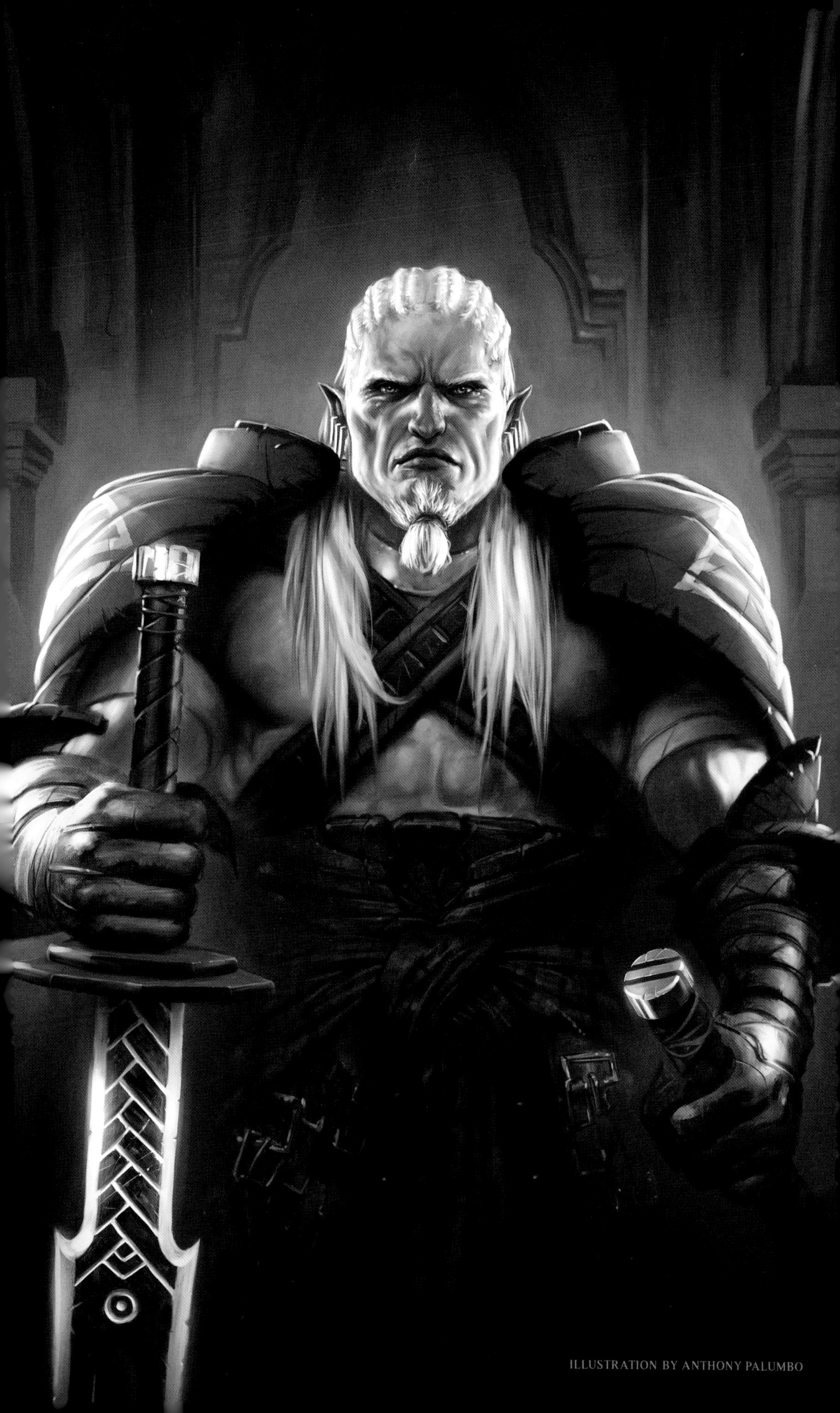

ILLUSTRATION BY ANTHONY PALUMBO

For nearly a decade, King Alistair of Ferelden has ruled with a steady hand, seeing to his homeland's reconstruction after the darkspawn blight. But when the words of a strange witch revealed that his father—King Maric—might still be alive, he set out to find Aurelian Titus, the mysterious mage responsible for Maric's disappearance.

But this story is not Alistair's alone.

The pirate Isabela has seen terrors across Thedas and plundered the ships and strongholds of the world's wealthiest merchants. Now the hired hand and confidante of King Alistair, she enjoys the luxury of a clean conscience—as well as steady pay for herself and her crew—on their journey to the North . . .

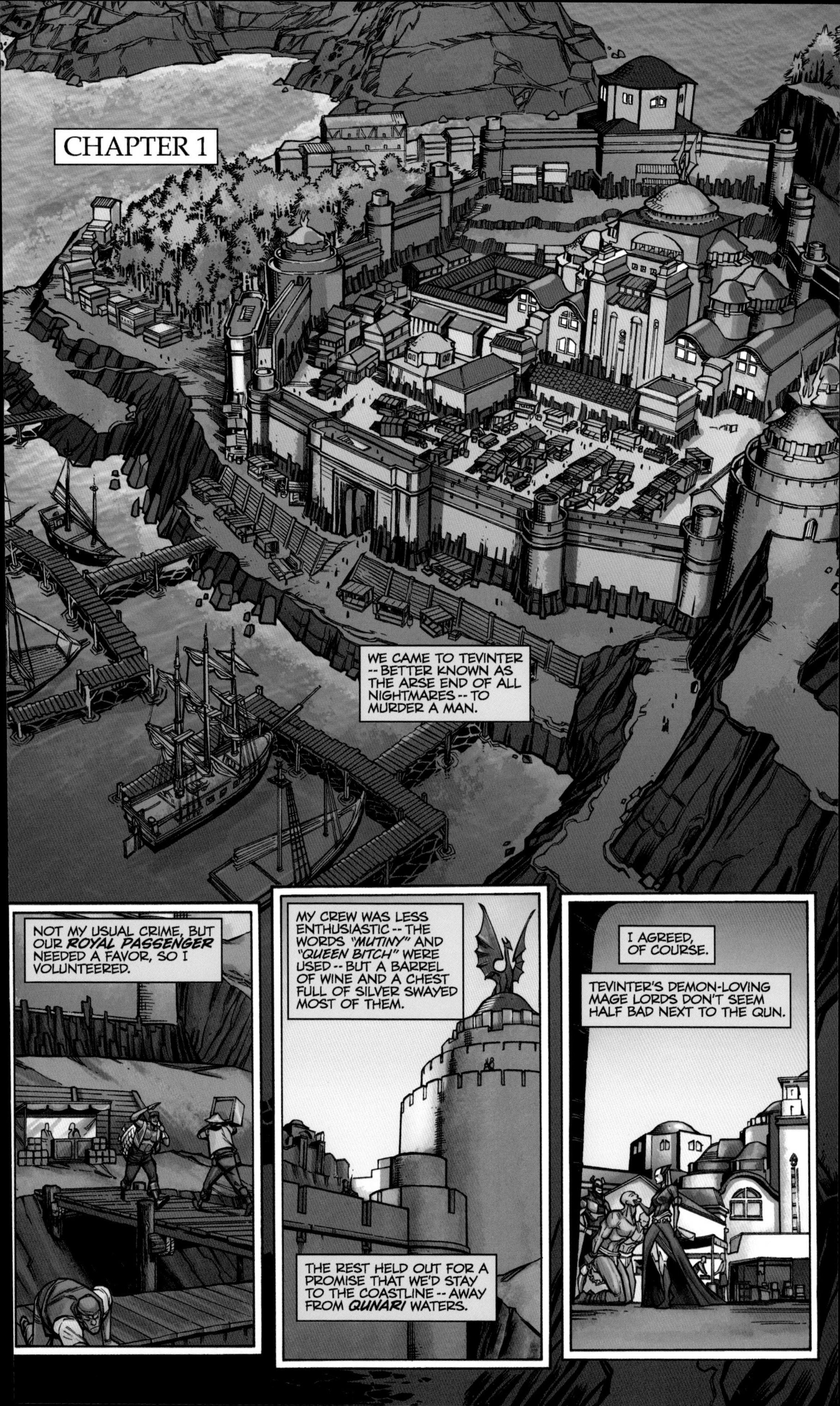
CHAPTER 1
WE CAME TO TEVINTER -- BETTER KNOWN AS THE ARSE END OF ALL NIGHTMARES -- TO MURDER A MAN.
NOT MY USUAL CRIME, BUT OUR *ROYAL PASSENGER* NEEDED A FAVOR, SO I VOLUNTEERED.
MY CREW WAS LESS ENTHUSIASTIC -- THE WORDS *"MUTINY"* AND *"QUEEN BITCH"* WERE USED -- BUT A BARREL OF WINE AND A CHEST FULL OF SILVER SWAYED MOST OF THEM.
THE REST HELD OUT FOR A PROMISE THAT WE'D STAY TO THE COASTLINE -- AWAY FROM *QUNARI* WATERS.
I AGREED, OF COURSE.
TEVINTER'S DEMON-LOVING MAGE LORDS DON'T SEEM HALF BAD NEXT TO THE QUN.

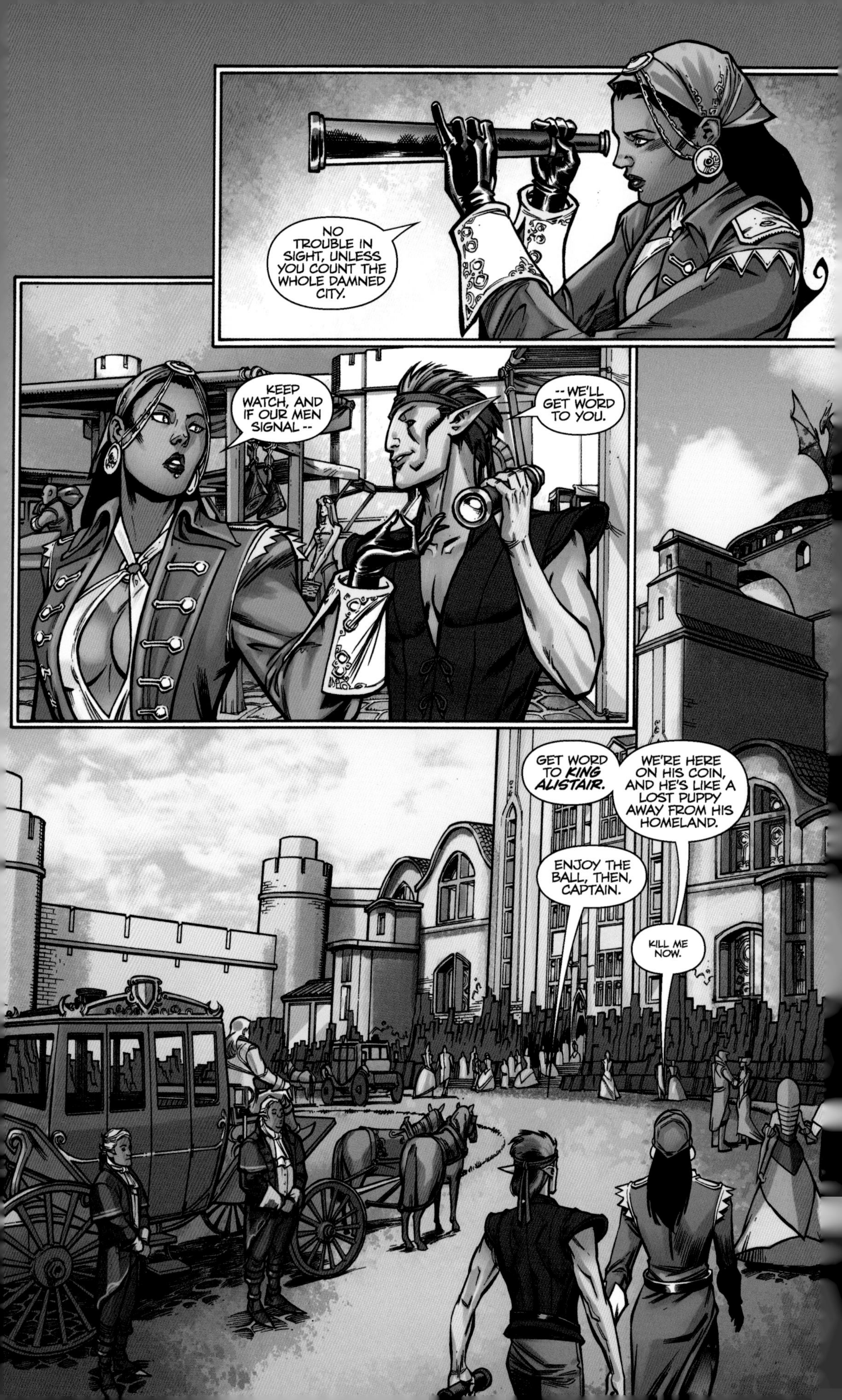
NO TROUBLE IN SIGHT, UNLESS YOU COUNT THE WHOLE DAMNED CITY.
KEEP WATCH, AND IF OUR MEN SIGNAL --
-- WE'LL GET WORD TO YOU.
GET WORD TO *KING ALISTAIR*.
WE'RE HERE ON HIS COIN, AND HE'S LIKE A LOST PUPPY AWAY FROM HIS HOMELAND.
ENJOY THE BALL, THEN, CAPTAIN.
KILL ME NOW.

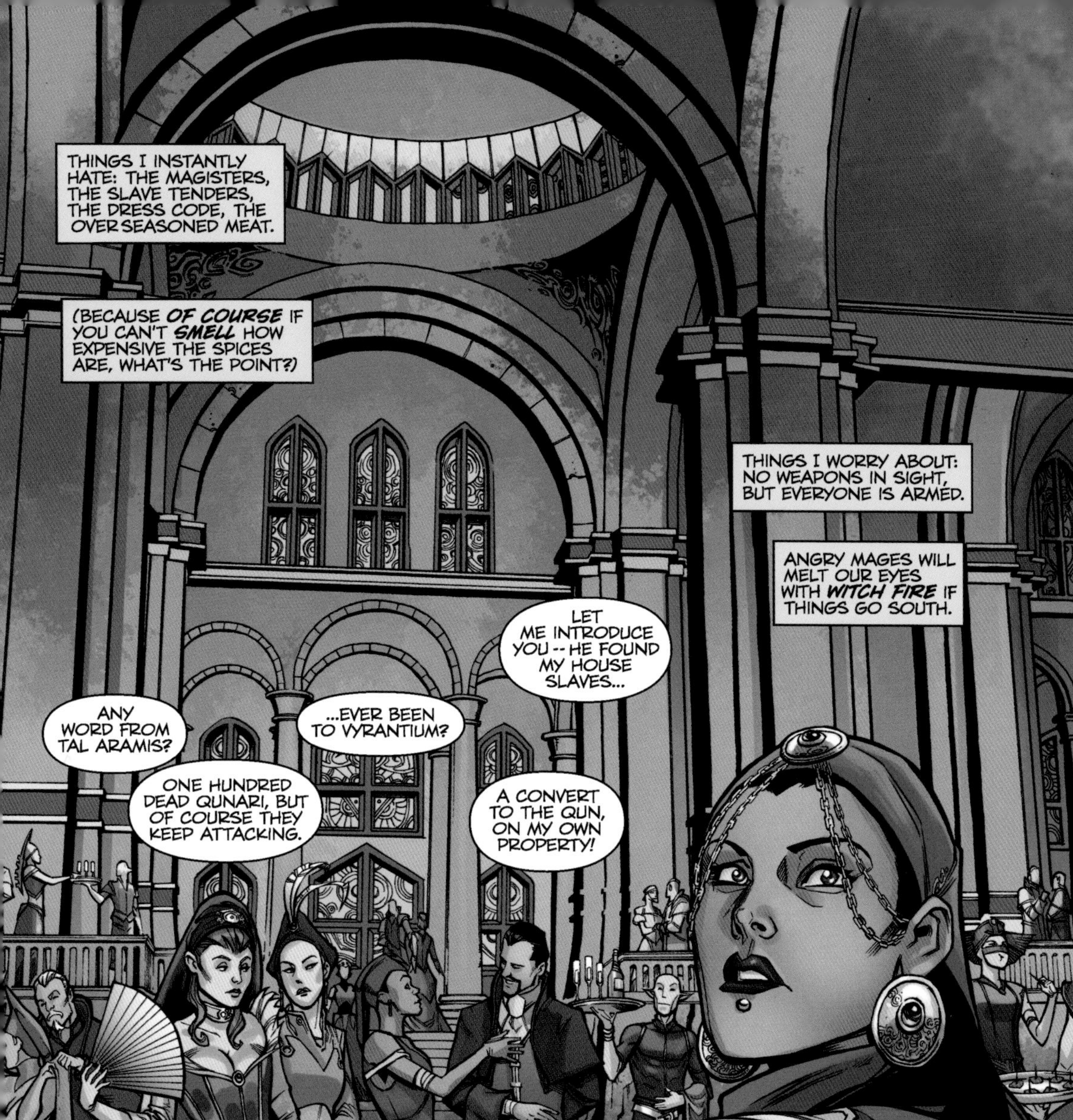
THINGS I INSTANTLY HATE: THE MAGISTERS, THE SLAVE TENDERS, THE DRESS CODE, THE OVERSEASONED MEAT.
(BECAUSE *OF COURSE* IF YOU CAN'T *SMELL* HOW EXPENSIVE THE SPICES ARE, WHAT'S THE POINT?)
THINGS I WORRY ABOUT: NO WEAPONS IN SIGHT, BUT EVERYONE IS ARMED.
ANGRY MAGES WILL MELT OUR EYES WITH *WITCH FIRE* IF THINGS GO SOUTH.
ANY WORD FROM TAL ARAMIS?
ONE HUNDRED DEAD QUNARI, BUT OF COURSE THEY KEEP ATTACKING.
...EVER BEEN TO VYRANTIUM?
LET ME INTRODUCE YOU -- HE FOUND MY HOUSE SLAVES...
A CONVERT TO THE QUN, ON MY OWN PROPERTY!

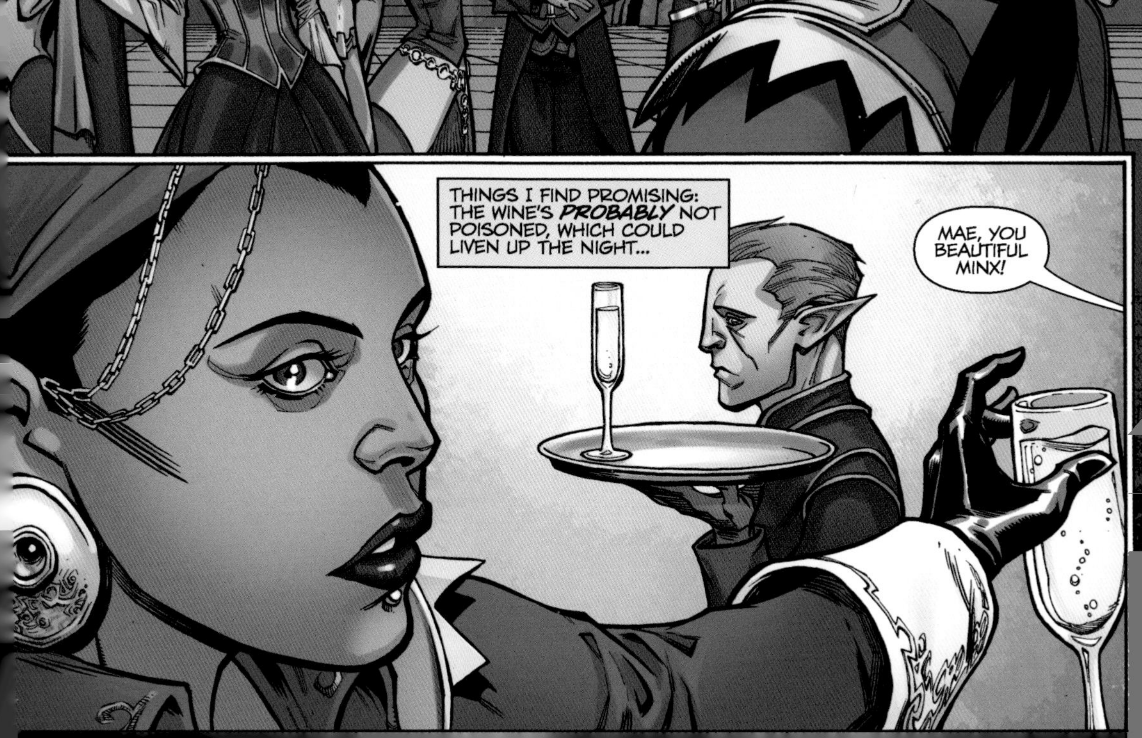
THINGS I FIND PROMISING: THE WINE'S *PROBABLY* NOT POISONED, WHICH COULD LIVEN UP THE NIGHT...
MAE, YOU BEAUTIFUL MINX!

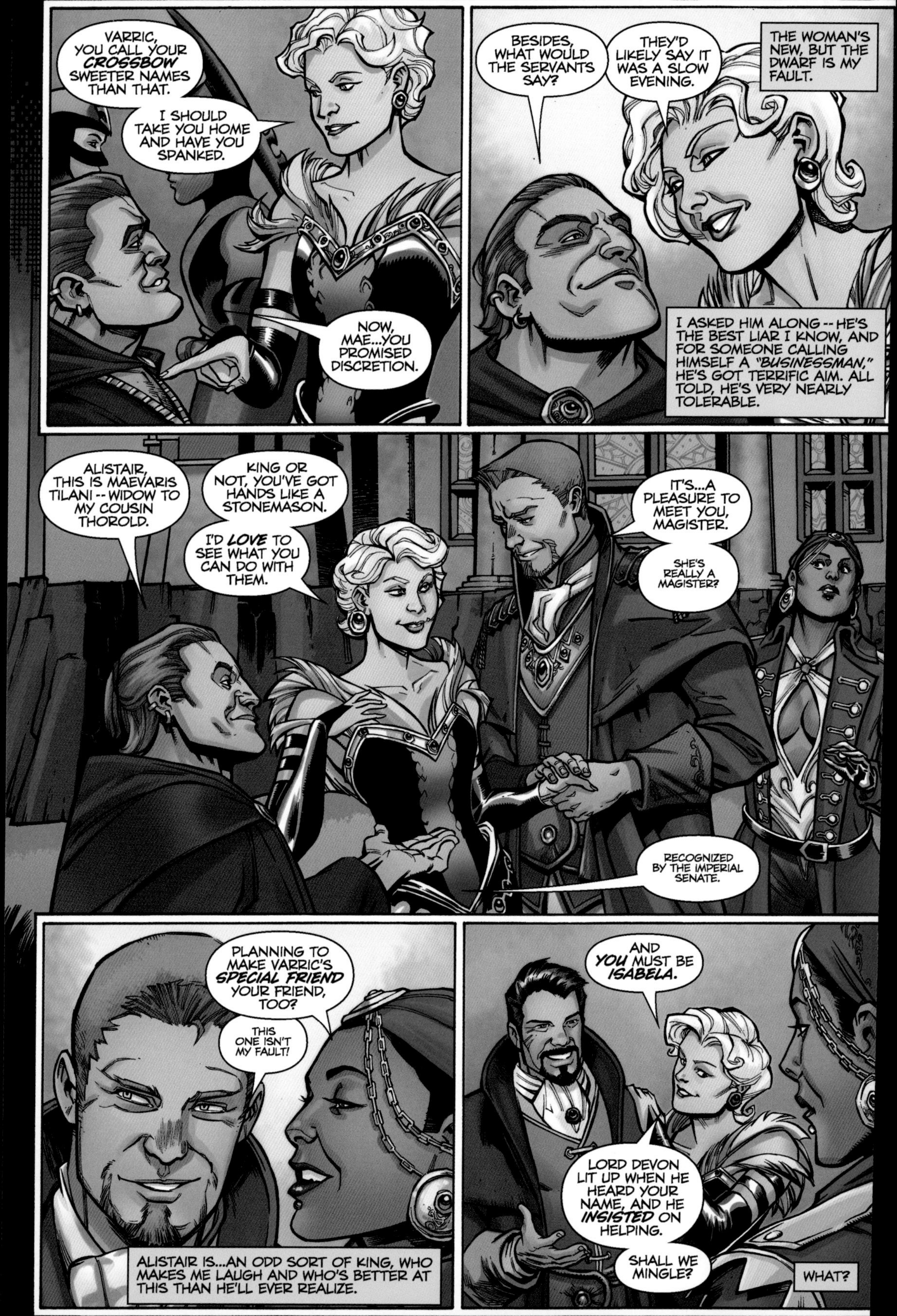

VARRIC, YOU CALL YOUR CROSSBOW SWEETER NAMES THAN THAT.
I SHOULD TAKE YOU HOME AND HAVE YOU SPANKED.
NOW, MAE...YOU PROMISED DISCRETION.
BESIDES, WHAT WOULD THE SERVANTS SAY?
THEY'D LIKELY SAY IT WAS A SLOW EVENING.
THE WOMAN'S NEW, BUT THE DWARF IS MY FAULT.
I ASKED HIM ALONG -- HE'S THE BEST LIAR I KNOW, AND FOR SOMEONE CALLING HIMSELF A "BUSINESSMAN," HE'S GOT TERRIFIC AIM. ALL TOLD, HE'S VERY NEARLY TOLERABLE.
ALISTAIR, THIS IS MAEVARIS TILANI -- WIDOW TO MY COUSIN THOROLD.
KING OR NOT, YOU'VE GOT HANDS LIKE A STONEMASON.
I'D LOVE TO SEE WHAT YOU CAN DO WITH THEM.
IT'S...A PLEASURE TO MEET YOU, MAGISTER.
SHE'S REALLY A MAGISTER?
RECOGNIZED BY THE IMPERIAL SENATE.
PLANNING TO MAKE VARRIC'S SPECIAL FRIEND YOUR FRIEND, TOO?
THIS ONE ISN'T MY FAULT!
ALISTAIR IS...AN ODD SORT OF KING, WHO MAKES ME LAUGH AND WHO'S BETTER AT THIS THAN HE'LL EVER REALIZE.
AND YOU MUST BE ISABELA.
LORD DEVON LIT UP WHEN HE HEARD YOUR NAME, AND HE INSISTED ON HELPING.
SHALL WE MINGLE?
WHAT?

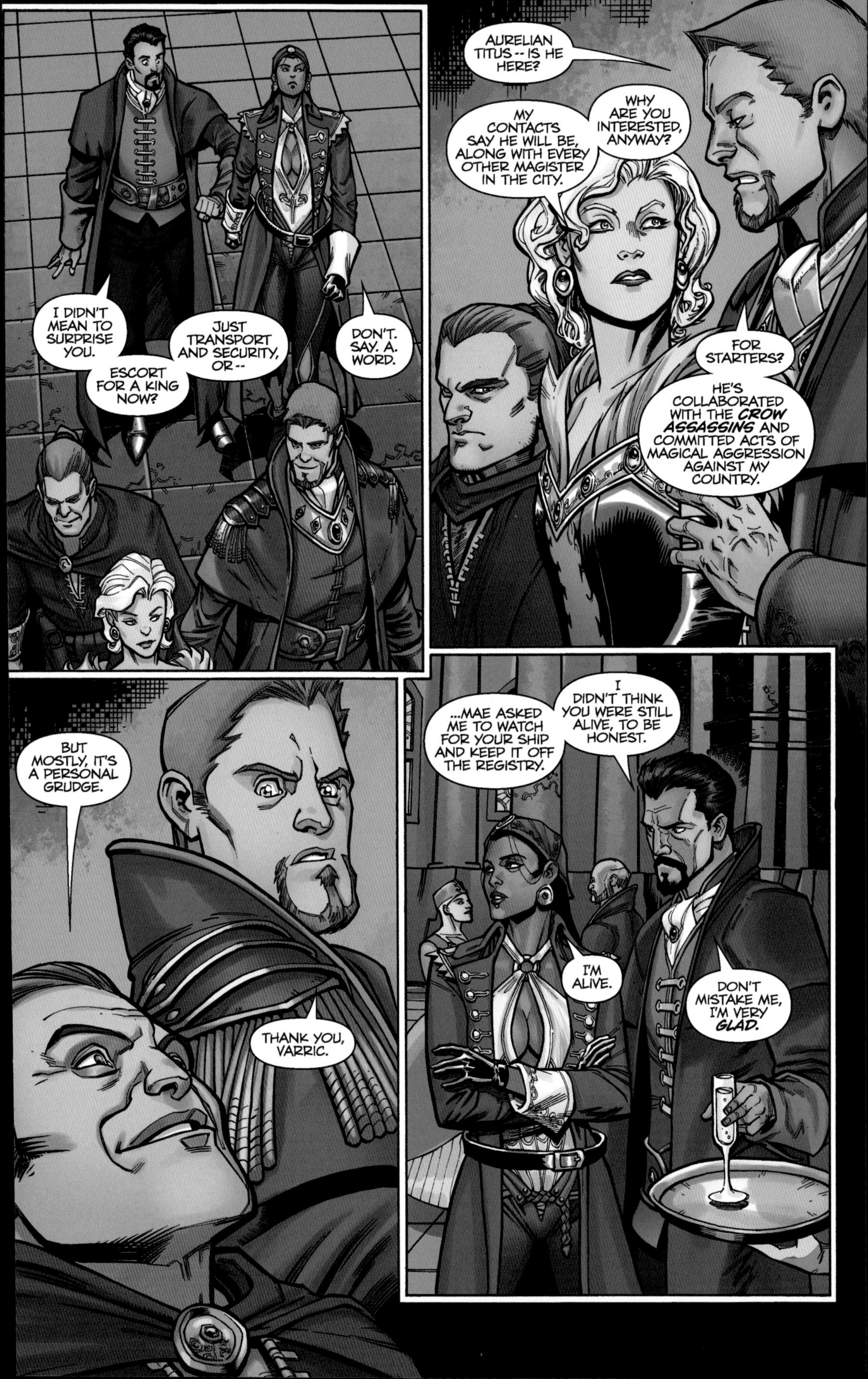
I DIDN'T MEAN TO SURPRISE YOU.
JUST TRANSPORT AND SECURITY, OR --
ESCORT FOR A KING NOW?
DON'T. SAY. A. WORD.
AURELIAN TITUS -- IS HE HERE?
MY CONTACTS SAY HE WILL BE, ALONG WITH EVERY OTHER MAGISTER IN THE CITY.
WHY ARE YOU INTERESTED, ANYWAY?
FOR STARTERS?
HE'S COLLABORATED WITH THE CROW ASSASSINS AND COMMITTED ACTS OF MAGICAL AGGRESSION AGAINST MY COUNTRY.
BUT MOSTLY, IT'S A PERSONAL GRUDGE.
THANK YOU, VARRIC.
...MAE ASKED ME TO WATCH FOR YOUR SHIP AND KEEP IT OFF THE REGISTRY.
I DIDN'T THINK YOU WERE STILL ALIVE, TO BE HONEST.
I'M ALIVE.
DON'T MISTAKE ME, I'M VERY GLAD.

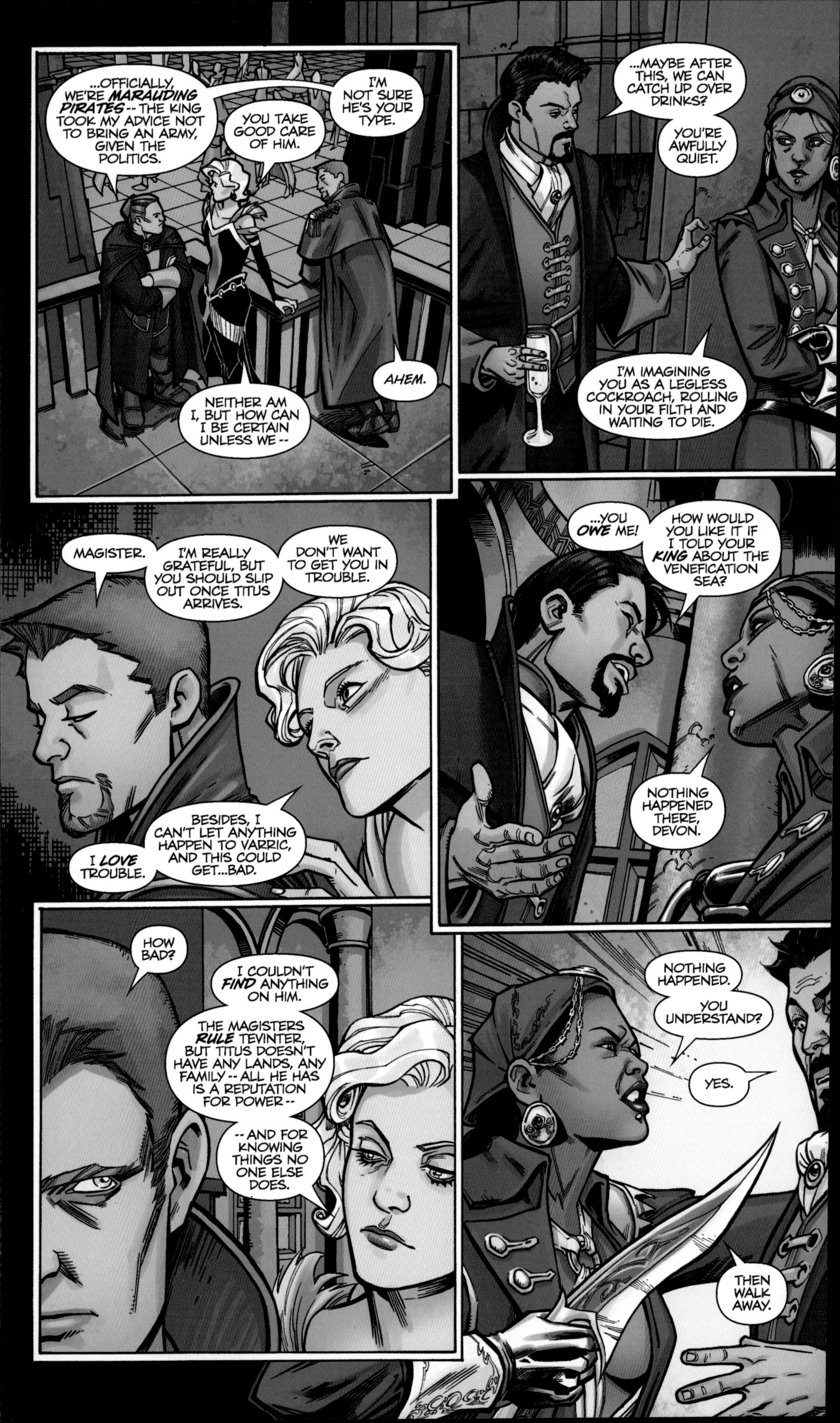

...OFFICIALLY, WE'RE MARAUDING PIRATES -- THE KING TOOK MY ADVICE NOT TO BRING AN ARMY, GIVEN THE POLITICS.
YOU TAKE GOOD CARE OF HIM.
I'M NOT SURE HE'S YOUR TYPE.
NEITHER AM I, BUT HOW CAN I BE CERTAIN UNLESS WE --
AHEM.
...MAYBE AFTER THIS, WE CAN CATCH UP OVER DRINKS?
YOU'RE AWFULLY QUIET.
I'M IMAGINING YOU AS A LEGLESS COCKROACH, ROLLING IN YOUR FILTH AND WAITING TO DIE.
MAGISTER.
I'M REALLY GRATEFUL, BUT YOU SHOULD SLIP OUT ONCE TITUS ARRIVES.
WE DON'T WANT TO GET YOU IN TROUBLE.
I LOVE TROUBLE.
BESIDES, I CAN'T LET ANYTHING HAPPEN TO VARRIC, AND THIS COULD GET...BAD.
...YOU OWE ME!
HOW WOULD YOU LIKE IT IF I TOLD YOUR KING ABOUT THE VENEFICATION SEA?
NOTHING HAPPENED THERE, DEVON.
HOW BAD?
I COULDN'T FIND ANYTHING ON HIM.
THE MAGISTERS RULE TEVINTER, BUT TITUS DOESN'T HAVE ANY LANDS, ANY FAMILY -- ALL HE HAS IS A REPUTATION FOR POWER --
-- AND FOR KNOWING THINGS NO ONE ELSE DOES.
NOTHING HAPPENED.
YOU UNDERSTAND?
YES.
THEN WALK AWAY.

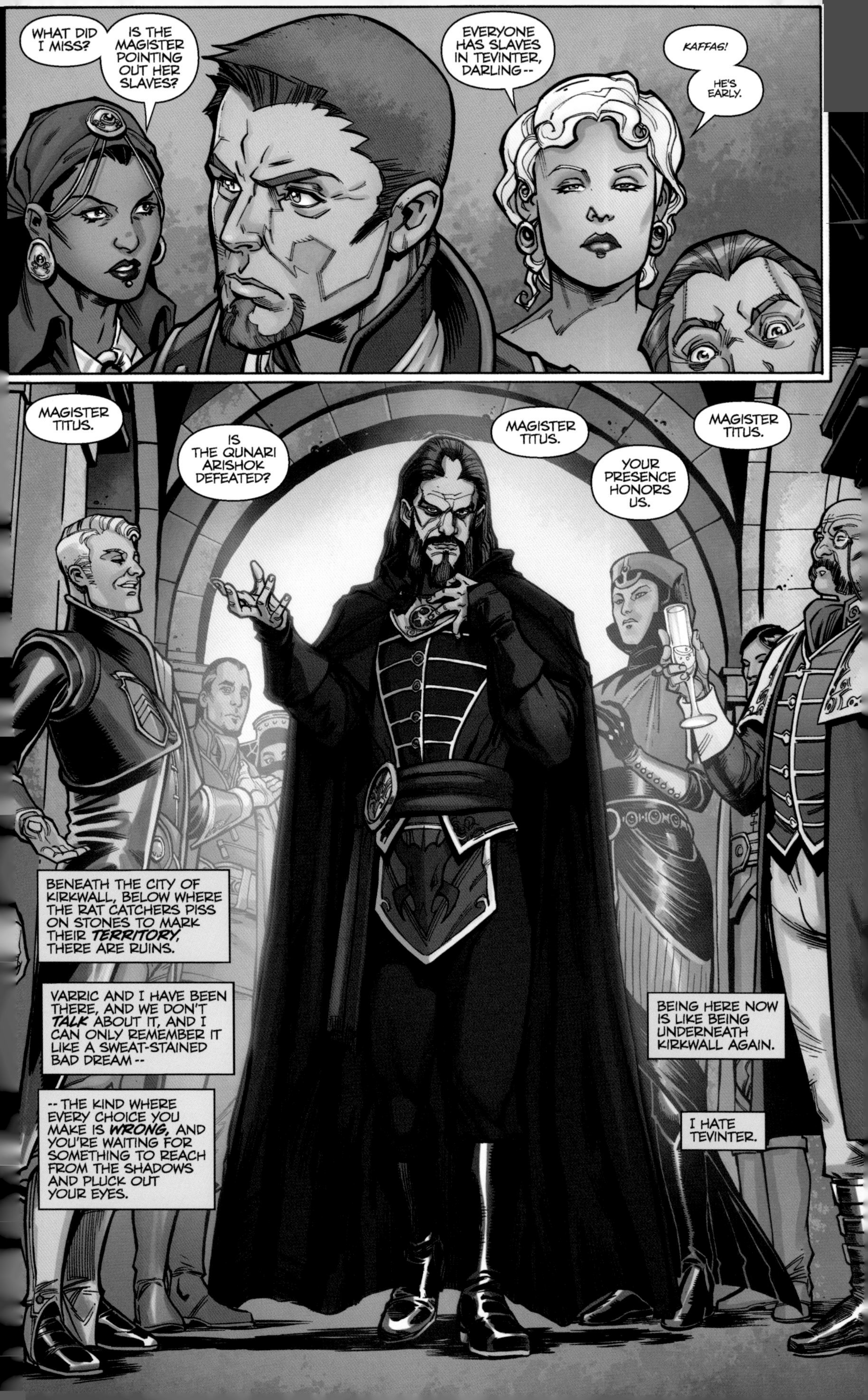

WHAT DID I MISS?
IS THE MAGISTER POINTING OUT HER SLAVES?
EVERYONE HAS SLAVES IN TEVINTER, DARLING --
KAFFAS!
HE'S EARLY.
MAGISTER TITUS.
IS THE QUNARI ARISHOK DEFEATED?
MAGISTER TITUS.
YOUR PRESENCE HONORS US.
MAGISTER TITUS.
BENEATH THE CITY OF KIRKWALL, BELOW WHERE THE RAT CATCHERS PISS ON STONES TO MARK THEIR TERRITORY, THERE ARE RUINS.
VARRIC AND I HAVE BEEN THERE, AND WE DON'T TALK ABOUT IT, AND I CAN ONLY REMEMBER IT LIKE A SWEAT-STAINED BAD DREAM --
-- THE KIND WHERE EVERY CHOICE YOU MAKE IS WRONG, AND YOU'RE WAITING FOR SOMETHING TO REACH FROM THE SHADOWS AND PLUCK OUT YOUR EYES.
BEING HERE NOW IS LIKE BEING UNDERNEATH KIRKWALL AGAIN.
I HATE TEVINTER.

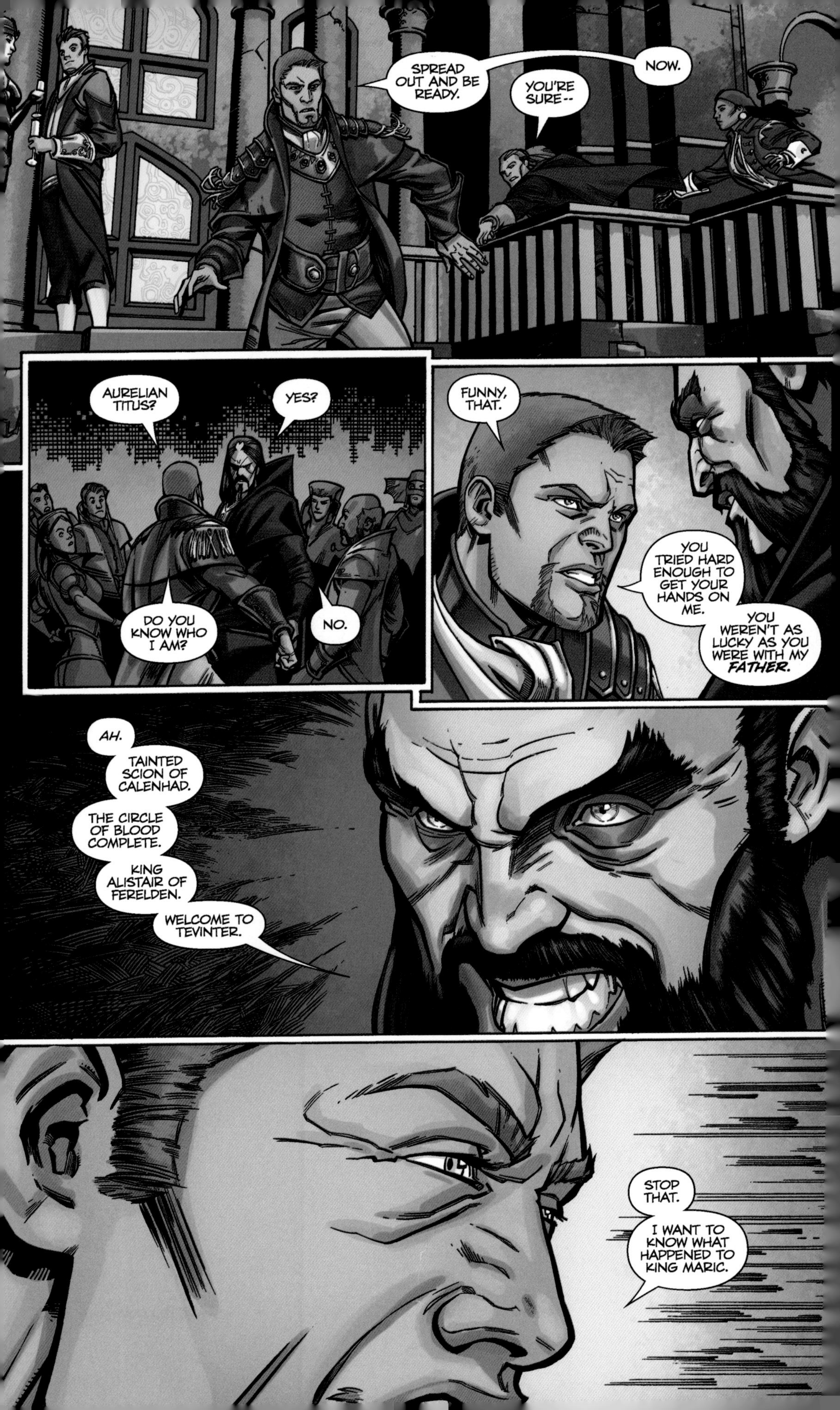
SPREAD OUT AND BE READY.
NOW.
YOU'RE SURE--
AURELIAN TITUS?
YES?
DO YOU KNOW WHO I AM?
NO.
FUNNY, THAT.
YOU TRIED HARD ENOUGH TO GET YOUR HANDS ON ME.
YOU WEREN'T AS LUCKY AS YOU WERE WITH MY *FATHER*.
AH.
TAINTED SCION OF CALENHAD.
THE CIRCLE OF BLOOD COMPLETE.
KING ALISTAIR OF FERELDEN.
WELCOME TO TEVINTER.
STOP THAT.
I WANT TO KNOW WHAT HAPPENED TO KING MARIC.

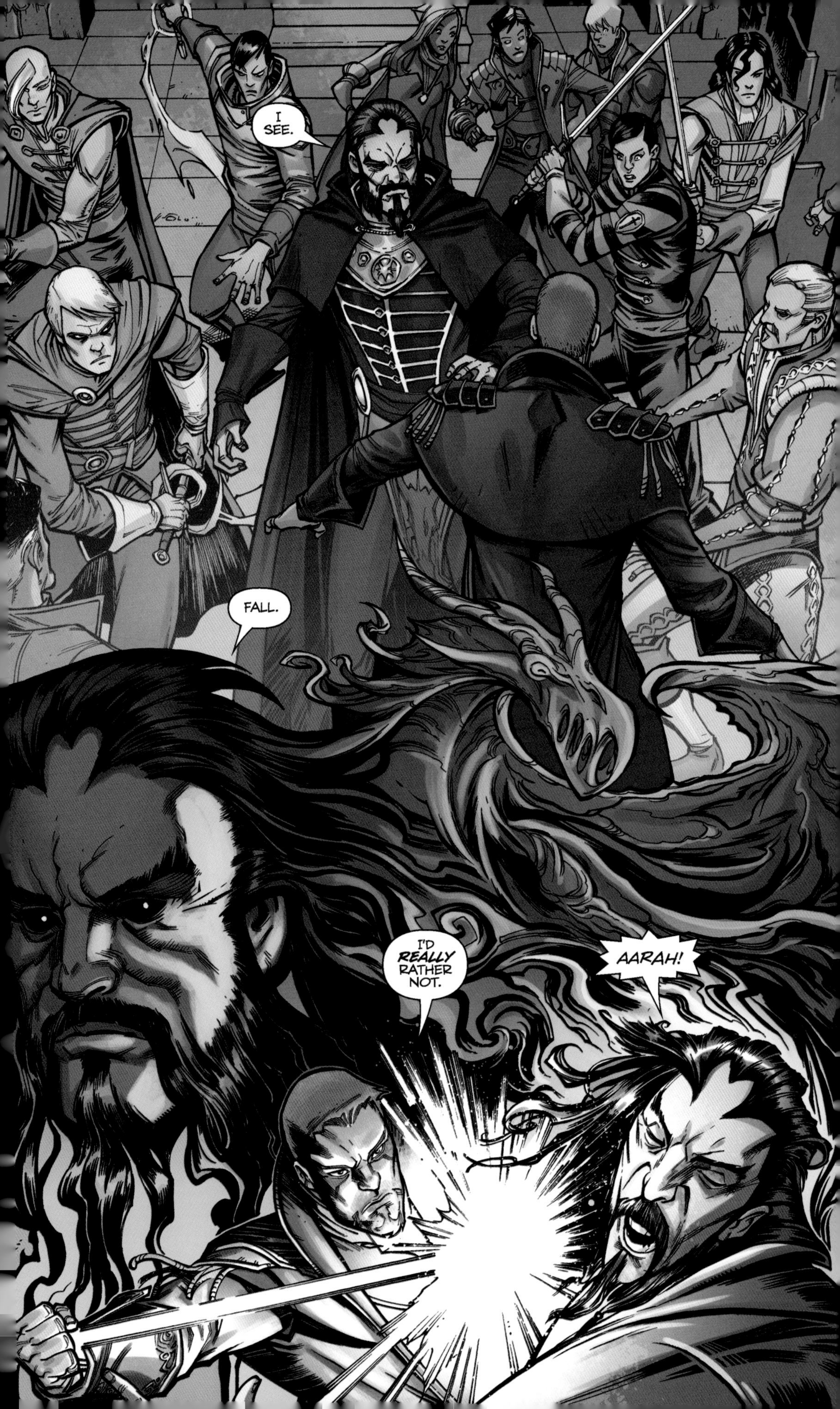
I SEE.
FALL.
I'D REALLY RATHER NOT.
AARAH!

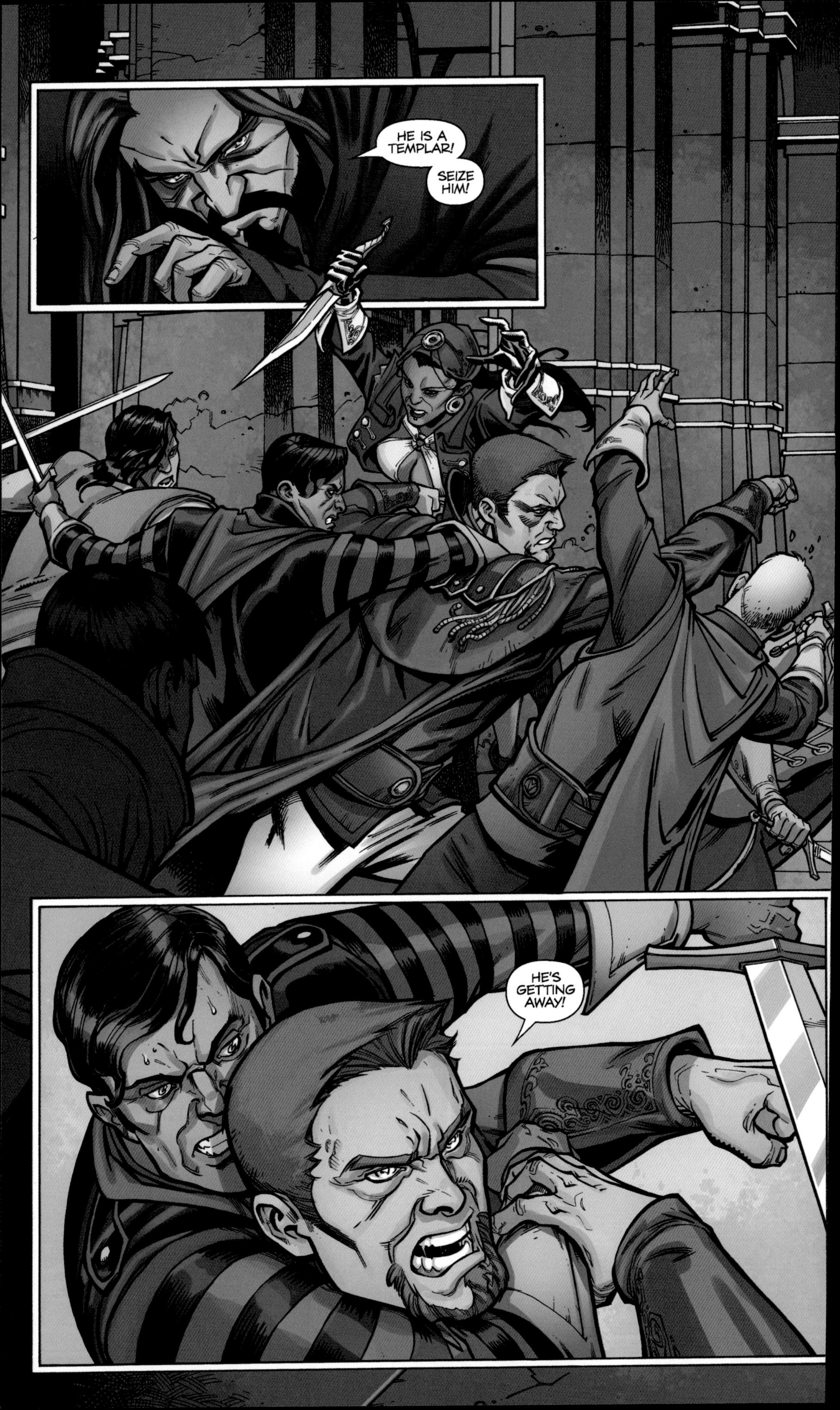
HE IS A TEMPLAR!
SEIZE HIM!
HE'S GETTING AWAY!

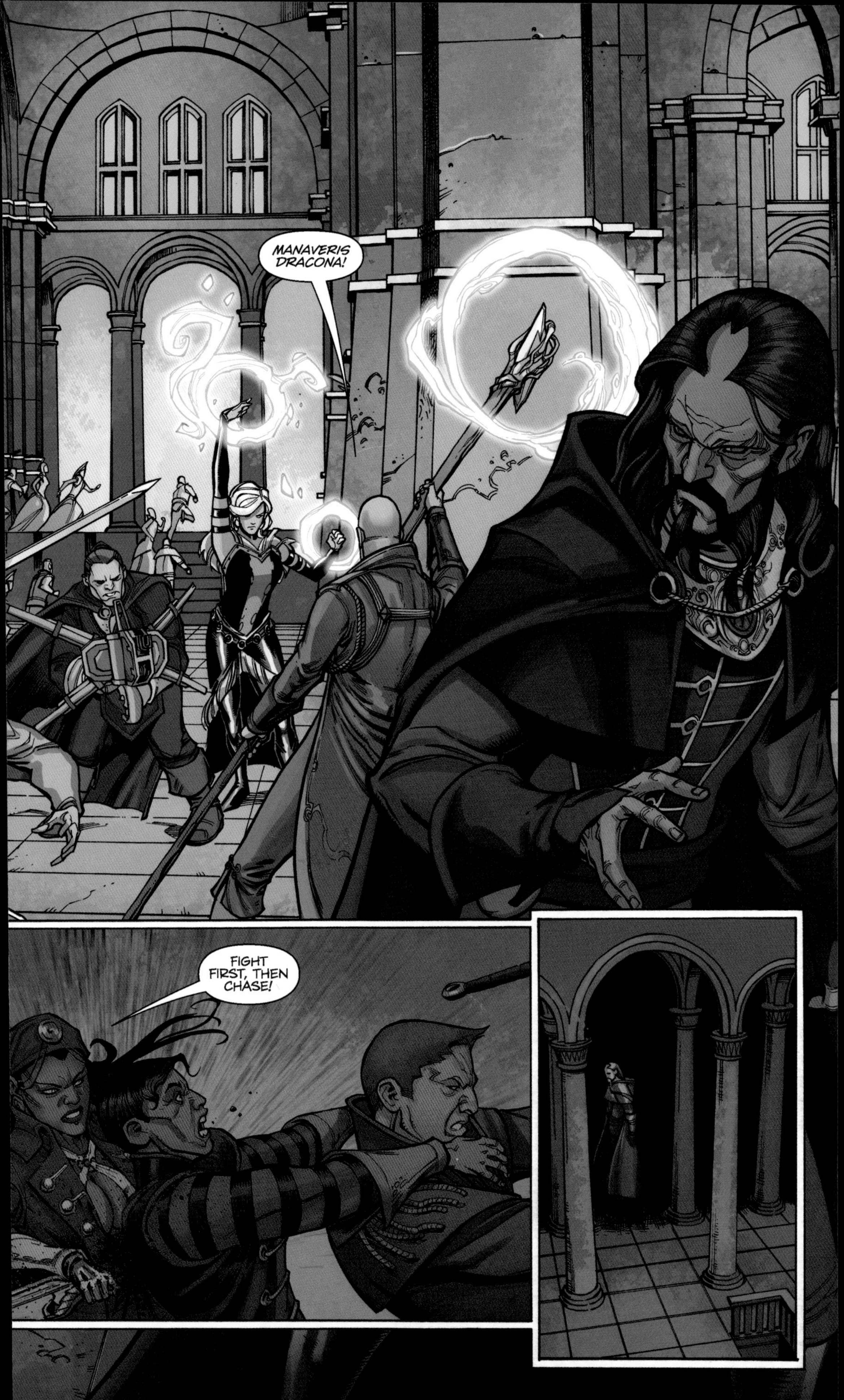
MANAVERIS DRACONA!
FIGHT FIRST, THEN CHASE!

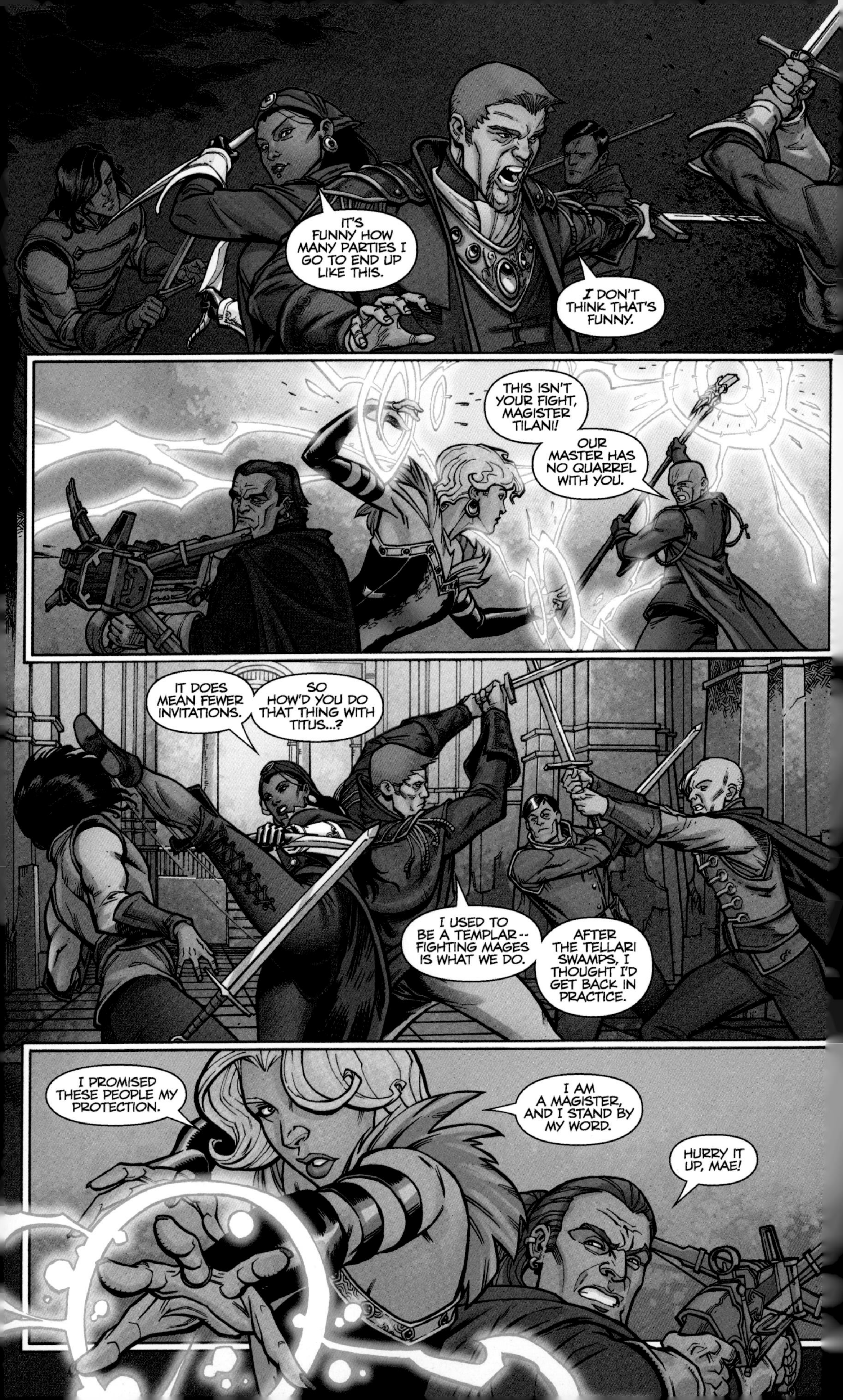
IT'S FUNNY HOW MANY PARTIES I GO TO END UP LIKE THIS.
I DON'T THINK THAT'S FUNNY.
THIS ISN'T YOUR FIGHT, MAGISTER TILANI!
OUR MASTER HAS NO QUARREL WITH YOU.
IT DOES MEAN FEWER INVITATIONS.
SO HOW'D YOU DO THAT THING WITH TITUS...?
I USED TO BE A TEMPLAR-- FIGHTING MAGES IS WHAT WE DO.
AFTER THE TELLARI SWAMPS, I THOUGHT I'D GET BACK IN PRACTICE.
I PROMISED THESE PEOPLE MY PROTECTION.
I AM A MAGISTER, AND I STAND BY MY WORD.
HURRY IT UP, MAE!

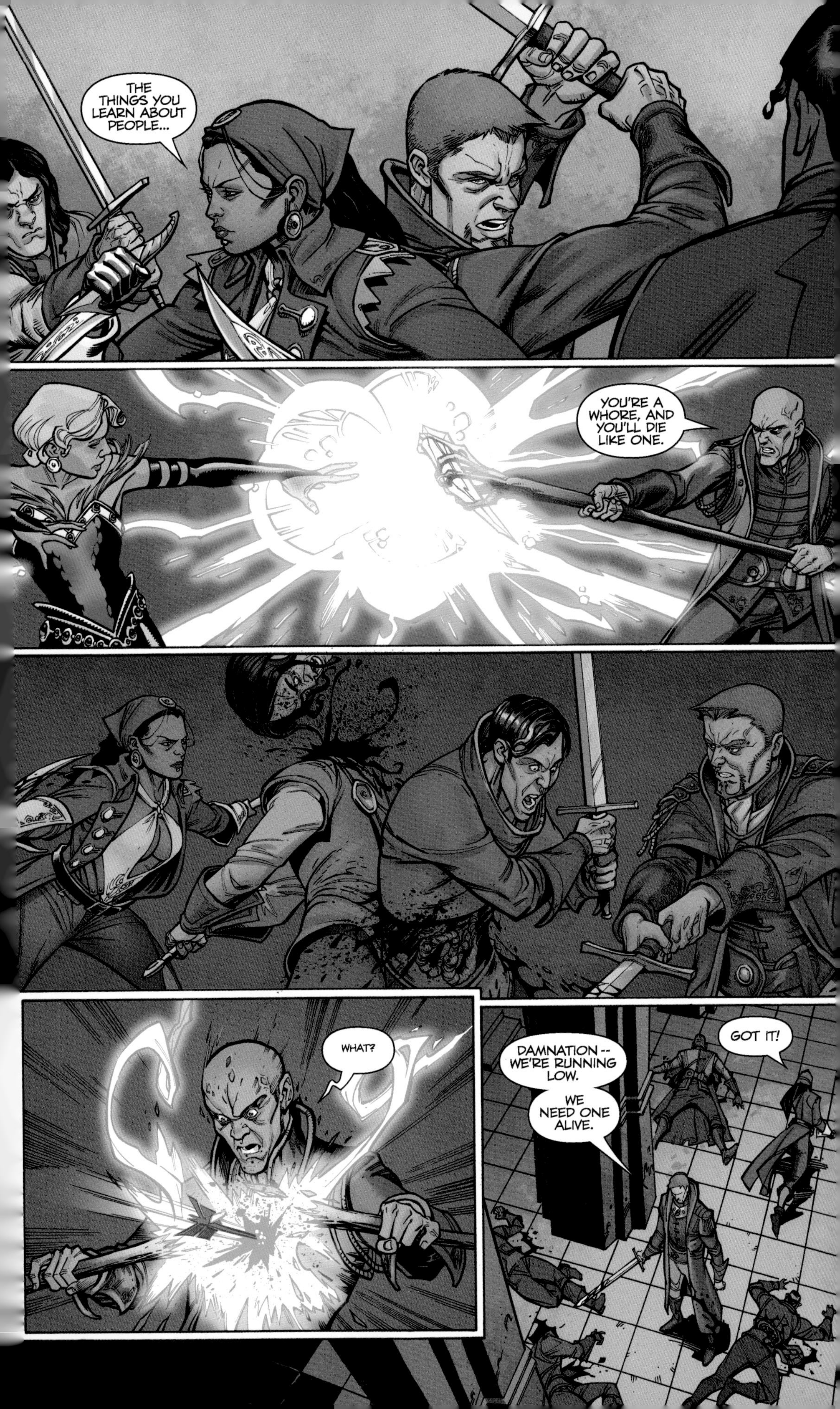
THE THINGS YOU LEARN ABOUT PEOPLE...
YOU'RE A WHORE, AND YOU'LL DIE LIKE ONE.
WHAT?
DAMNATION -- WE'RE RUNNING LOW.
WE NEED ONE ALIVE.
GOT IT!

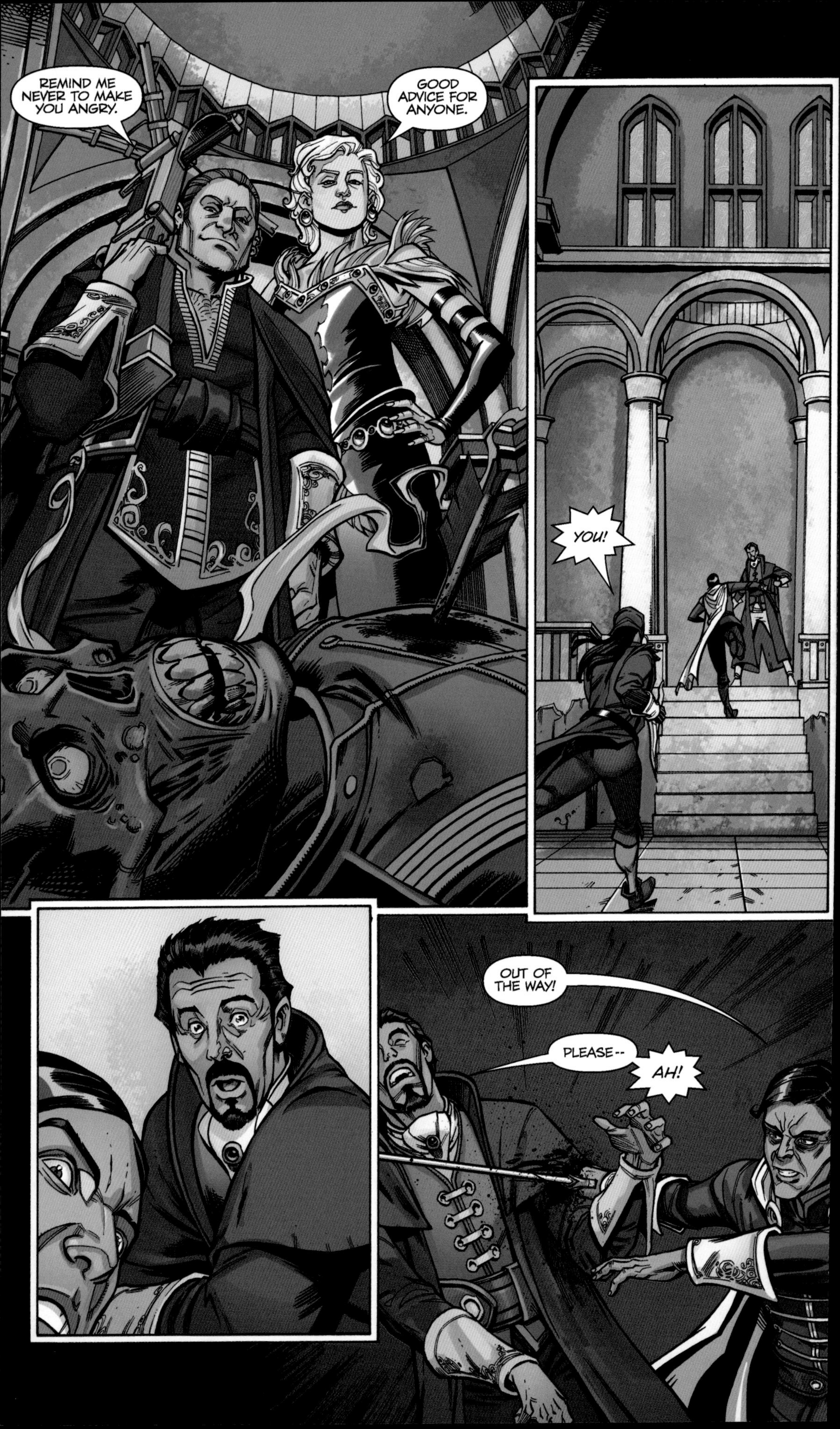
REMIND ME NEVER TO MAKE YOU ANGRY.
GOOD ADVICE FOR ANYONE.
YOU!
OUT OF THE WAY!
PLEASE--
AH!

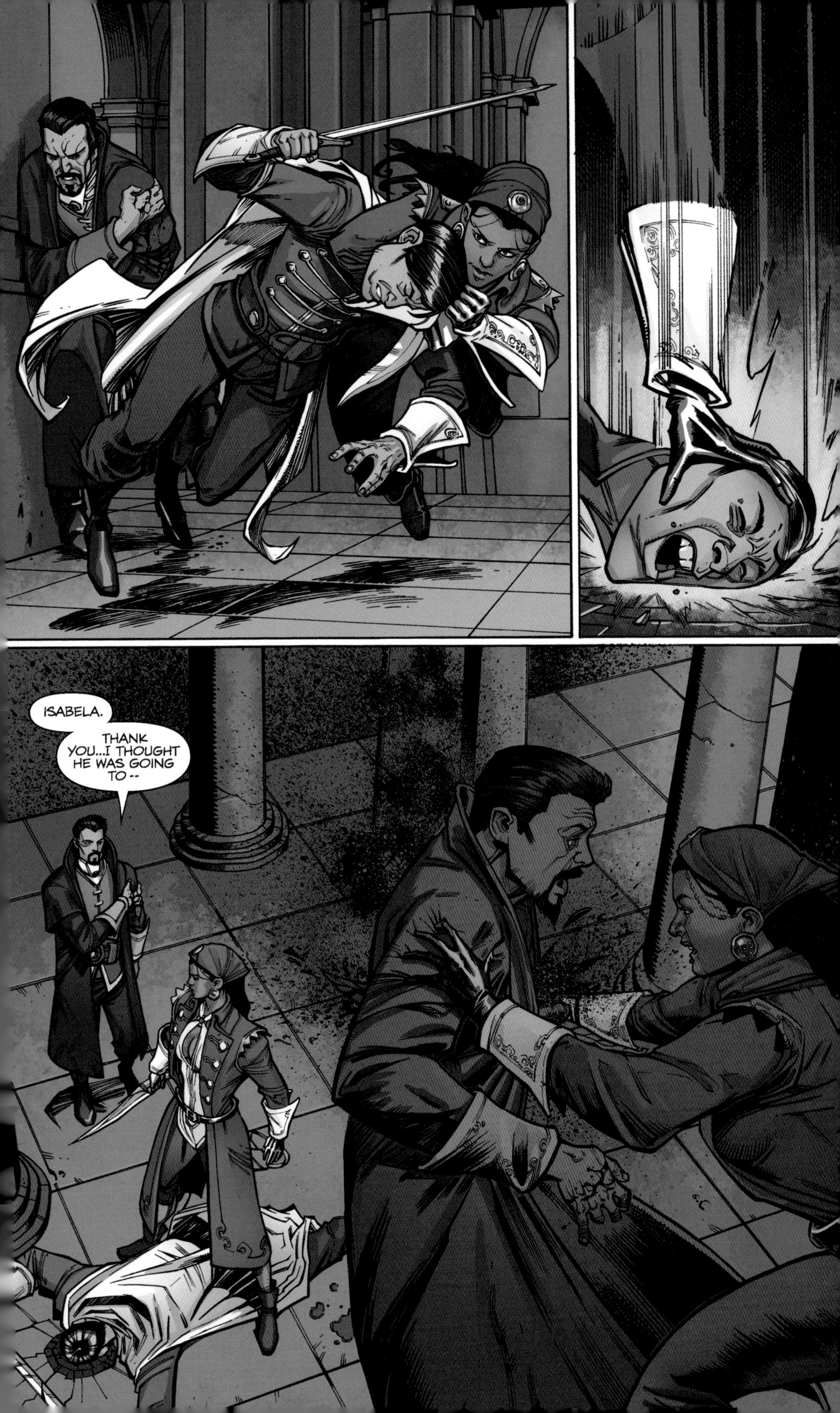
ISABELA.
THANK YOU...I THOUGHT HE WAS GOING TO --

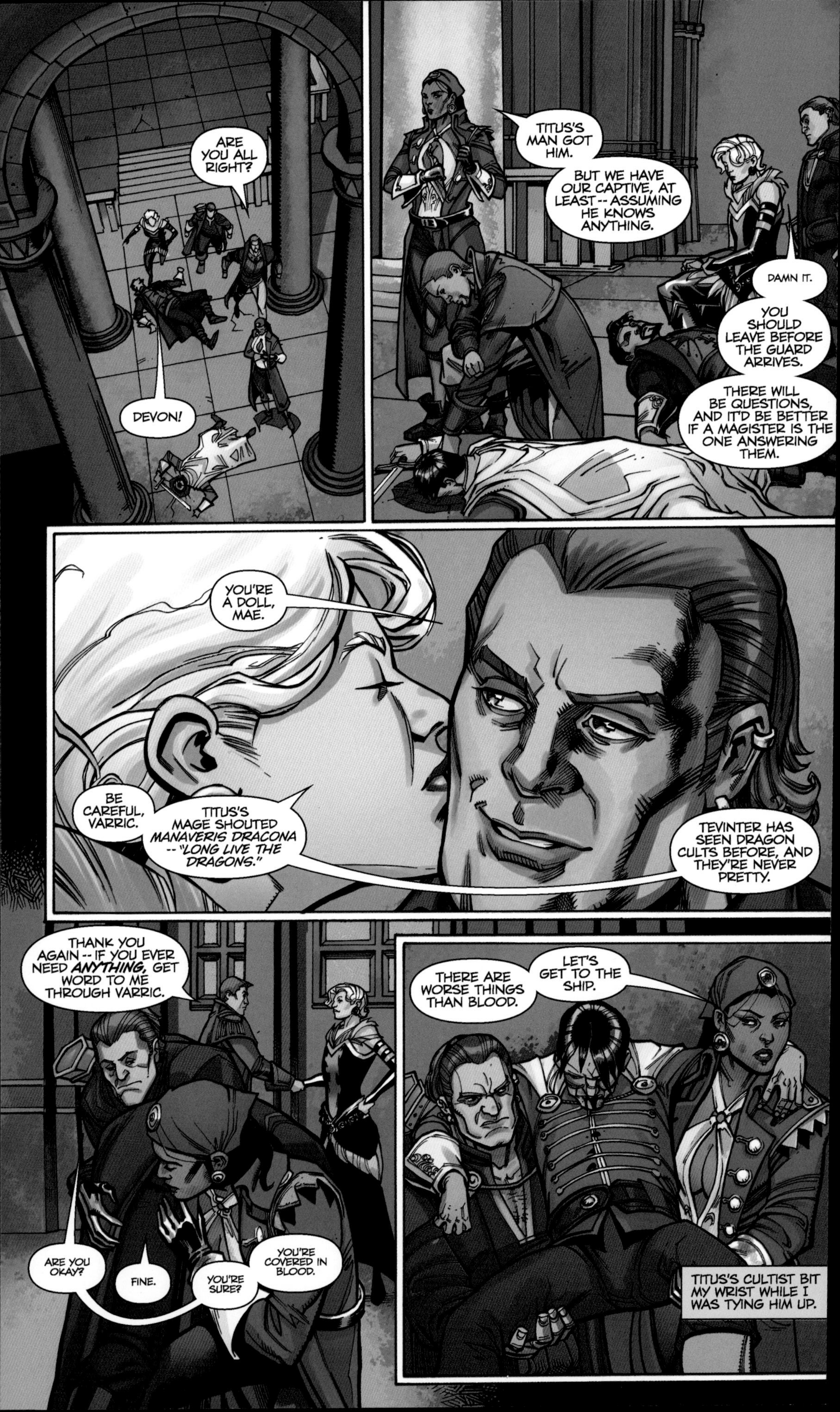
ARE YOU ALL RIGHT?
DEVON!
TITUS'S MAN GOT HIM.
BUT WE HAVE OUR CAPTIVE, AT LEAST -- ASSUMING HE KNOWS ANYTHING.
DAMN IT.
YOU SHOULD LEAVE BEFORE THE GUARD ARRIVES.
THERE WILL BE QUESTIONS, AND IT'D BE BETTER IF A MAGISTER IS THE ONE ANSWERING THEM.
YOU'RE A DOLL, MAE.
BE CAREFUL, VARRIC.
TITUS'S MAGE SHOUTED *MANAVERIS DRACONA* -- *"LONG LIVE THE DRAGONS."*
TEVINTER HAS SEEN DRAGON CULTS BEFORE, AND THEY'RE NEVER PRETTY.
THANK YOU AGAIN -- IF YOU EVER NEED *ANYTHING*, GET WORD TO ME THROUGH VARRIC.
ARE YOU OKAY?
FINE.
YOU'RE SURE?
YOU'RE COVERED IN BLOOD.
THERE ARE WORSE THINGS THAN BLOOD.
LET'S GET TO THE SHIP.
TITUS'S CULTIST BIT MY WRIST WHILE I WAS TYING HIM UP.

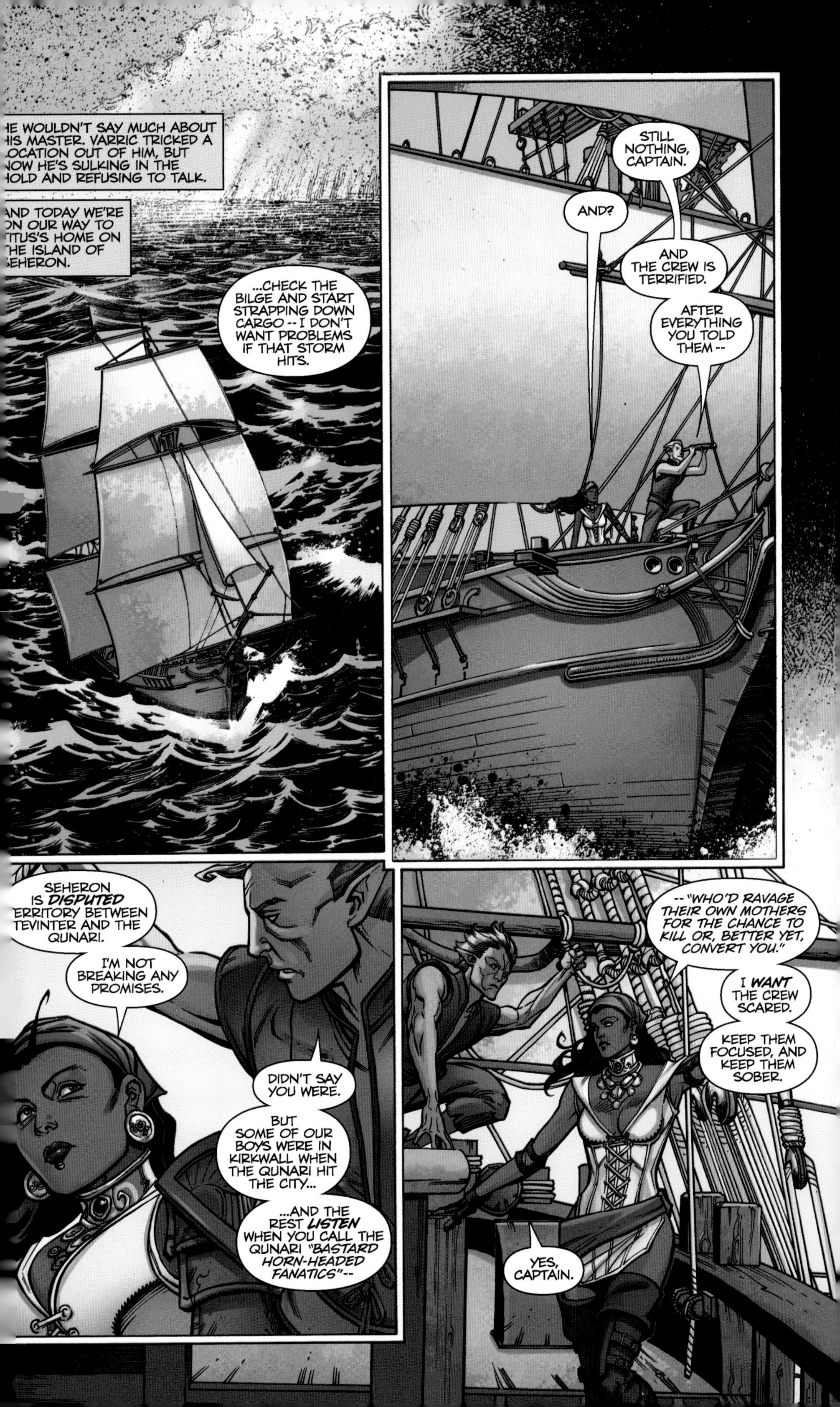
HE WOULDN'T SAY MUCH ABOUT HIS MASTER. VARRIC TRICKED A LOCATION OUT OF HIM, BUT NOW HE'S SULKING IN THE HOLD AND REFUSING TO TALK.
AND TODAY WE'RE ON OUR WAY TO TITUS'S HOME ON THE ISLAND OF SEHERON.
...CHECK THE BILGE AND START STRAPPING DOWN CARGO -- I DON'T WANT PROBLEMS IF THAT STORM HITS.
STILL NOTHING, CAPTAIN.
AND?
AND THE CREW IS TERRIFIED.
AFTER EVERYTHING YOU TOLD THEM --
SEHERON IS DISPUTED TERRITORY BETWEEN TEVINTER AND THE QUNARI.
I'M NOT BREAKING ANY PROMISES.
DIDN'T SAY YOU WERE.
BUT SOME OF OUR BOYS WERE IN KIRKWALL WHEN THE QUNARI HIT THE CITY...
...AND THE REST LISTEN WHEN YOU CALL THE QUNARI "BASTARD HORN-HEADED FANATICS"--
-- "WHO'D RAVAGE THEIR OWN MOTHERS FOR THE CHANCE TO KILL OR, BETTER YET, CONVERT YOU."
I WANT THE CREW SCARED.
KEEP THEM FOCUSED, AND KEEP THEM SOBER.
YES, CAPTAIN.

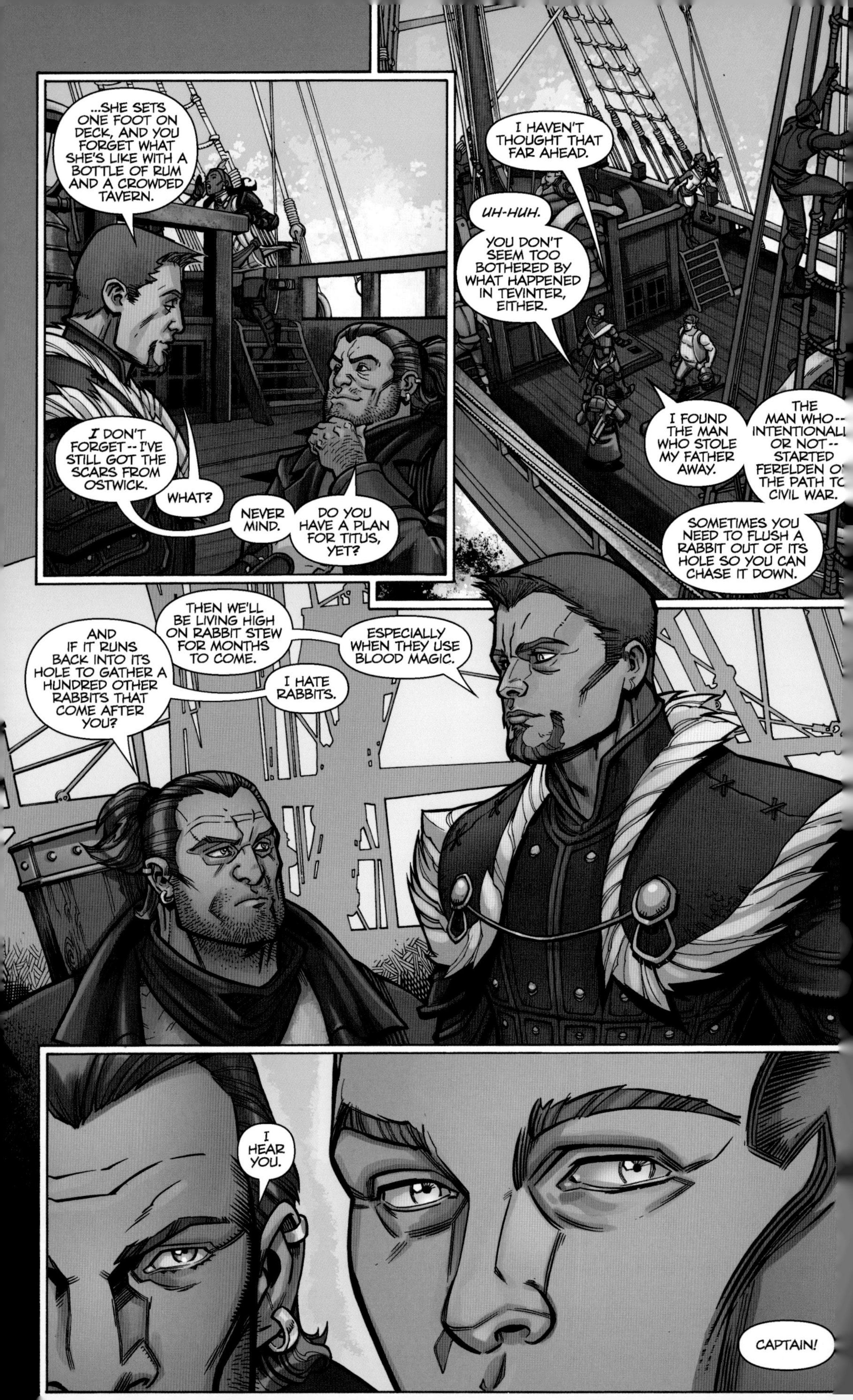
...SHE SETS ONE FOOT ON DECK, AND YOU FORGET WHAT SHE'S LIKE WITH A BOTTLE OF RUM AND A CROWDED TAVERN.
I DON'T FORGET -- I'VE STILL GOT THE SCARS FROM OSTWICK.
WHAT?
NEVER MIND.
DO YOU HAVE A PLAN FOR TITUS, YET?
I HAVEN'T THOUGHT THAT FAR AHEAD.
UH-HUH.
YOU DON'T SEEM TOO BOTHERED BY WHAT HAPPENED IN TEVINTER, EITHER.
I FOUND THE MAN WHO STOLE MY FATHER AWAY.
THE MAN WHO-- INTENTIONALL OR NOT-- STARTED FERELDEN O THE PATH TO CIVIL WAR.
SOMETIMES YOU NEED TO FLUSH A RABBIT OUT OF ITS HOLE SO YOU CAN CHASE IT DOWN.
AND IF IT RUNS BACK INTO ITS HOLE TO GATHER A HUNDRED OTHER RABBITS THAT COME AFTER YOU?
THEN WE'LL BE LIVING HIGH ON RABBIT STEW FOR MONTHS TO COME.
ESPECIALLY WHEN THEY USE BLOOD MAGIC.
I HATE RABBITS.
I HEAR YOU.
CAPTAIN!

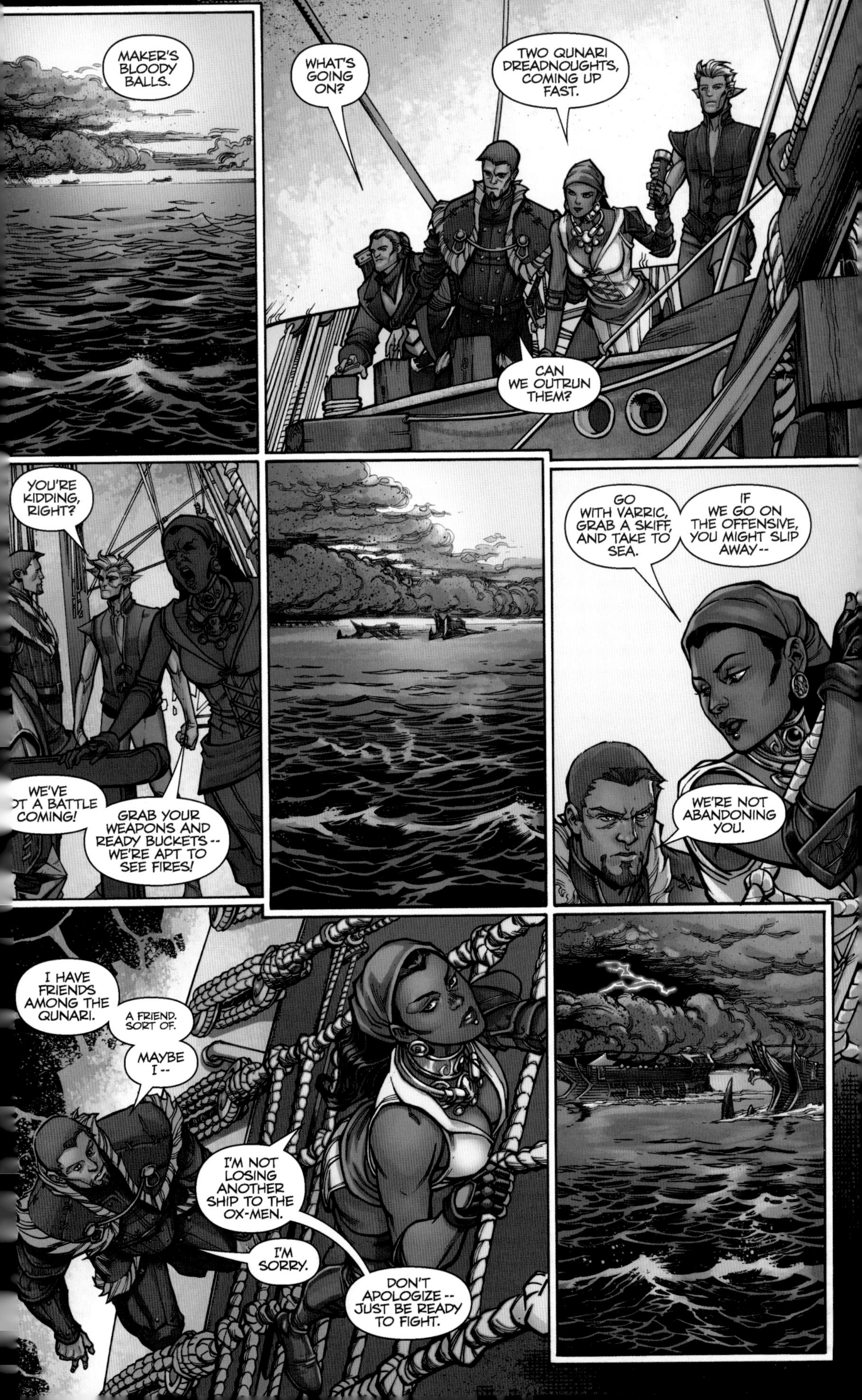
MAKER'S BLOODY BALLS.
WHAT'S GOING ON?
TWO QUNARI DREADNOUGHTS, COMING UP FAST.
CAN WE OUTRUN THEM?
YOU'RE KIDDING, RIGHT?
WE'VE GOT A BATTLE COMING!
GRAB YOUR WEAPONS AND READY BUCKETS -- WE'RE APT TO SEE FIRES!
IF WE GO ON THE OFFENSIVE, YOU MIGHT SLIP AWAY--
GO WITH VARRIC, GRAB A SKIFF, AND TAKE TO SEA.
WE'RE NOT ABANDONING YOU.
I HAVE FRIENDS AMONG THE QUNARI.
A FRIEND. SORT OF.
MAYBE I --
I'M NOT LOSING ANOTHER SHIP TO THE OX-MEN.
I'M SORRY.
DON'T APOLOGIZE -- JUST BE READY TO FIGHT.

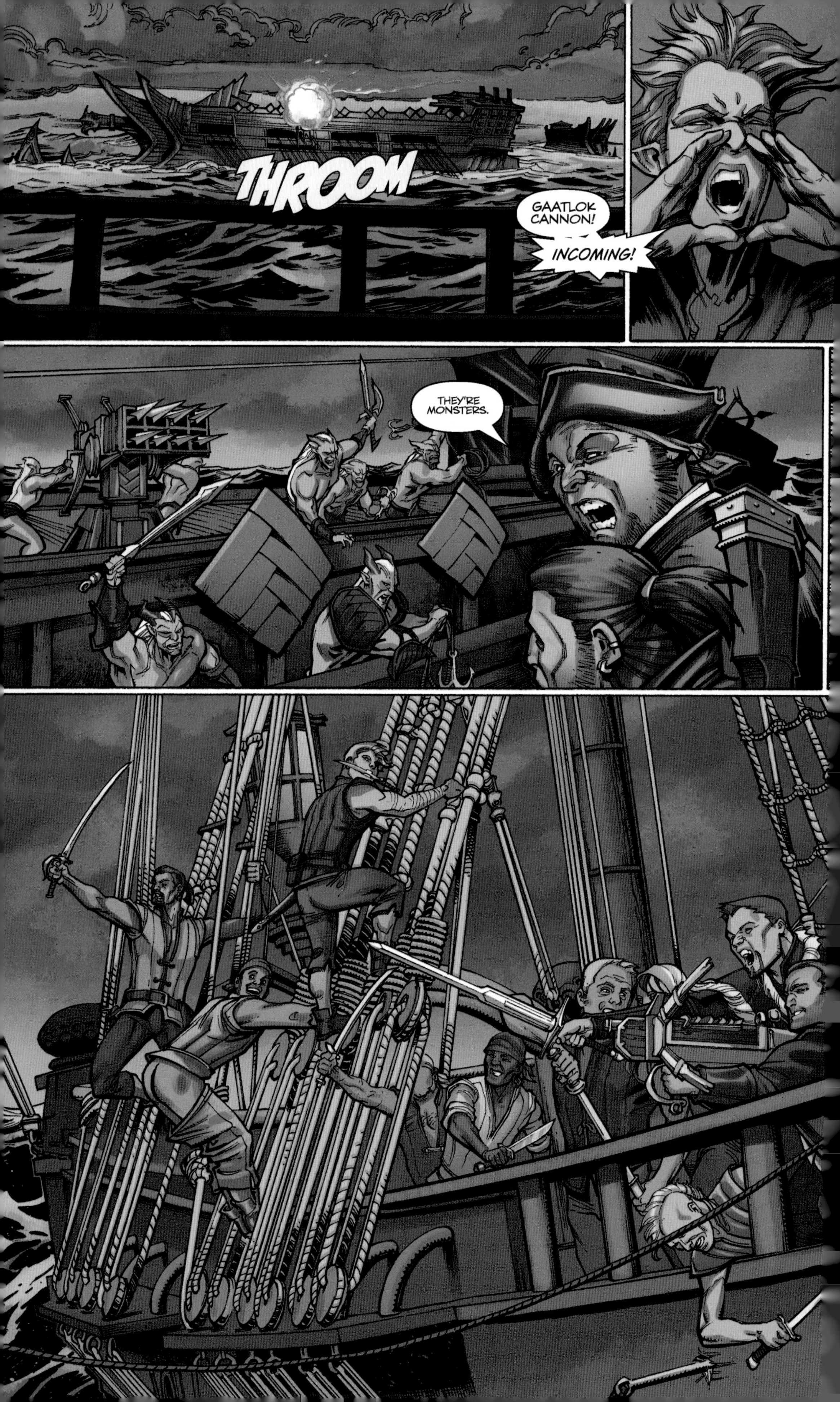
THROOM
GAATLOK CANNON!
INCOMING!
THEY'RE MONSTERS.

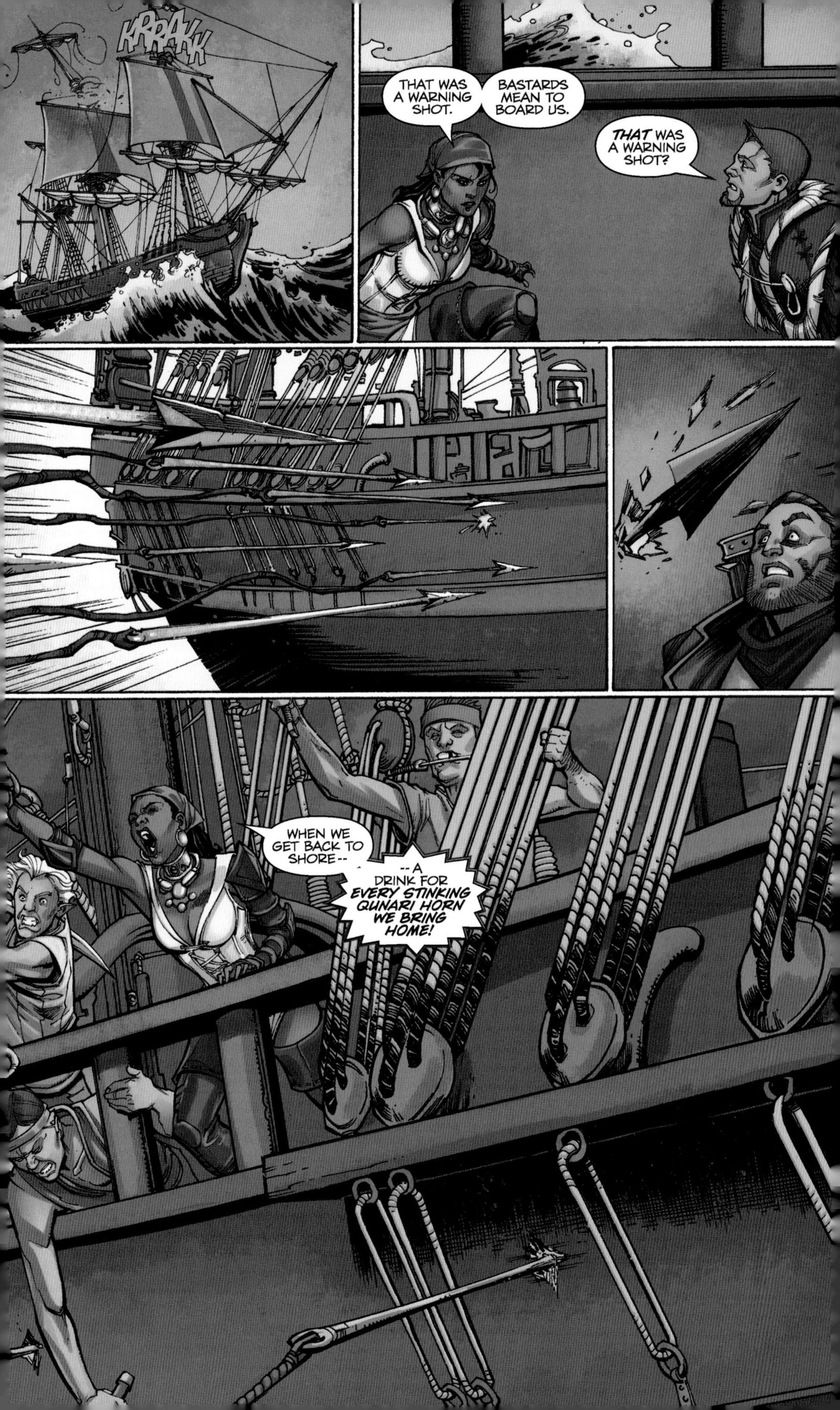
KRRAKK
THAT WAS A WARNING SHOT.
BASTARDS MEAN TO BOARD US.
THAT WAS A WARNING SHOT?
WHEN WE GET BACK TO SHORE--
--A DRINK FOR EVERY STINKING QUNARI HORN WE BRING HOME!

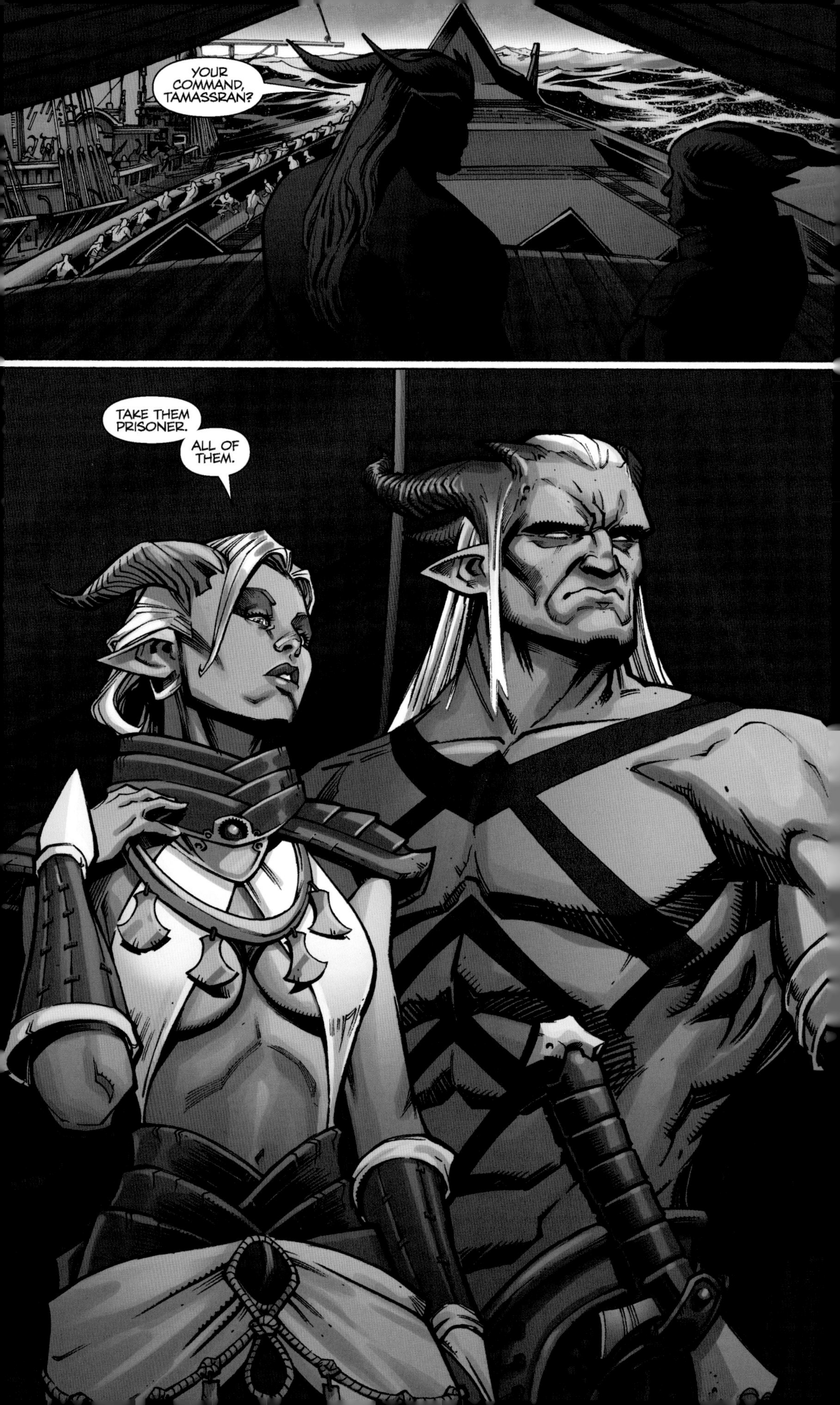
YOUR COMMAND, TAMASSRAN?
TAKE THEM PRISONER.
ALL OF THEM.

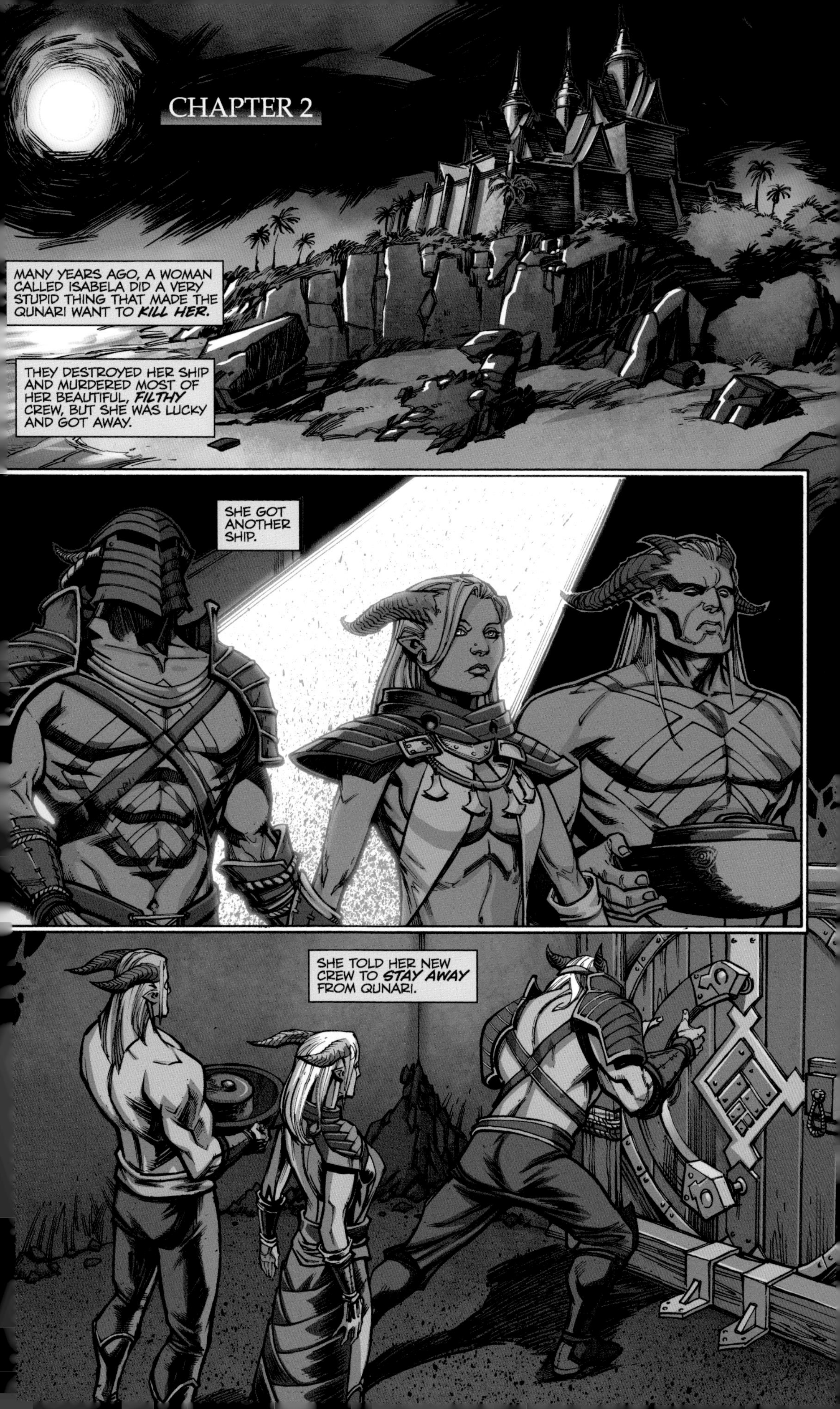
CHAPTER 2
MANY YEARS AGO, A WOMAN CALLED ISABELA DID A VERY STUPID THING THAT MADE THE QUNARI WANT TO KILL HER.
THEY DESTROYED HER SHIP AND MURDERED MOST OF HER BEAUTIFUL, FILTHY CREW, BUT SHE WAS LUCKY AND GOT AWAY.
SHE GOT ANOTHER SHIP.
SHE TOLD HER NEW CREW TO STAY AWAY FROM QUNARI.

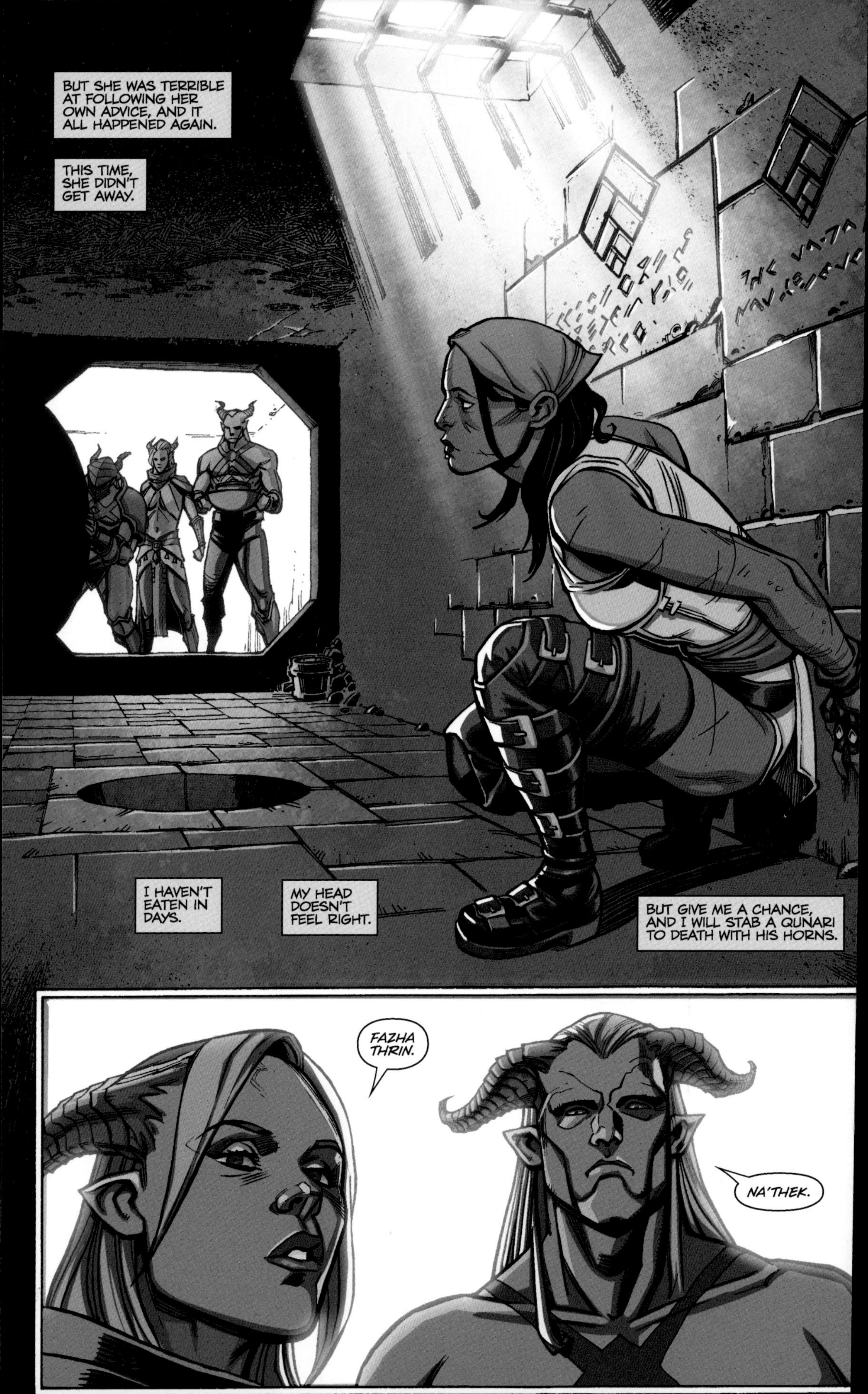
BUT SHE WAS TERRIBLE AT FOLLOWING HER OWN ADVICE, AND IT ALL HAPPENED AGAIN.
THIS TIME, SHE DIDN'T GET AWAY.
I HAVEN'T EATEN IN DAYS.
MY HEAD DOESN'T FEEL RIGHT.
BUT GIVE ME A CHANCE, AND I WILL STAB A QUNARI TO DEATH WITH HIS HORNS.
FAZHA THRIN.
NA'THEK.

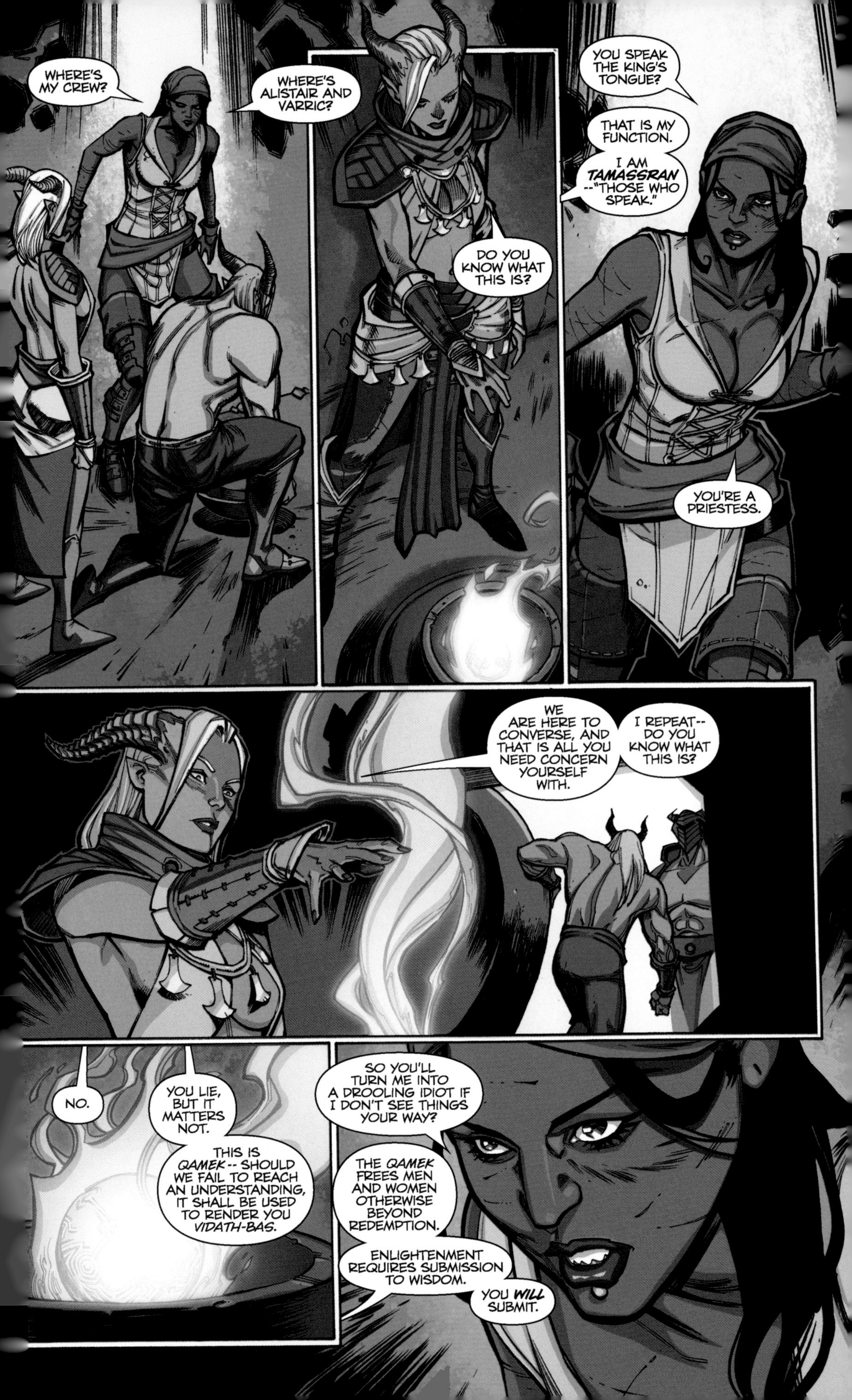
WHERE'S MY CREW?
WHERE'S ALISTAIR AND VARRIC?
DO YOU KNOW WHAT THIS IS?
YOU SPEAK THE KING'S TONGUE?
THAT IS MY FUNCTION.
I AM *TAMASSRAN* --"THOSE WHO SPEAK."
YOU'RE A PRIESTESS.
WE ARE HERE TO CONVERSE, AND THAT IS ALL YOU NEED CONCERN YOURSELF WITH.
I REPEAT-- DO YOU KNOW WHAT THIS IS?
NO.
YOU LIE, BUT IT MATTERS NOT.
THIS IS *QAMEK* -- SHOULD WE FAIL TO REACH AN UNDERSTANDING, IT SHALL BE USED TO RENDER YOU *VIDATH-BAS*.
SO YOU'LL TURN ME INTO A DROOLING IDIOT IF I DON'T SEE THINGS YOUR WAY?
THE *QAMEK* FREES MEN AND WOMEN OTHERWISE BEYOND REDEMPTION.
ENLIGHTENMENT REQUIRES SUBMISSION TO WISDOM.
YOU **WILL** SUBMIT.

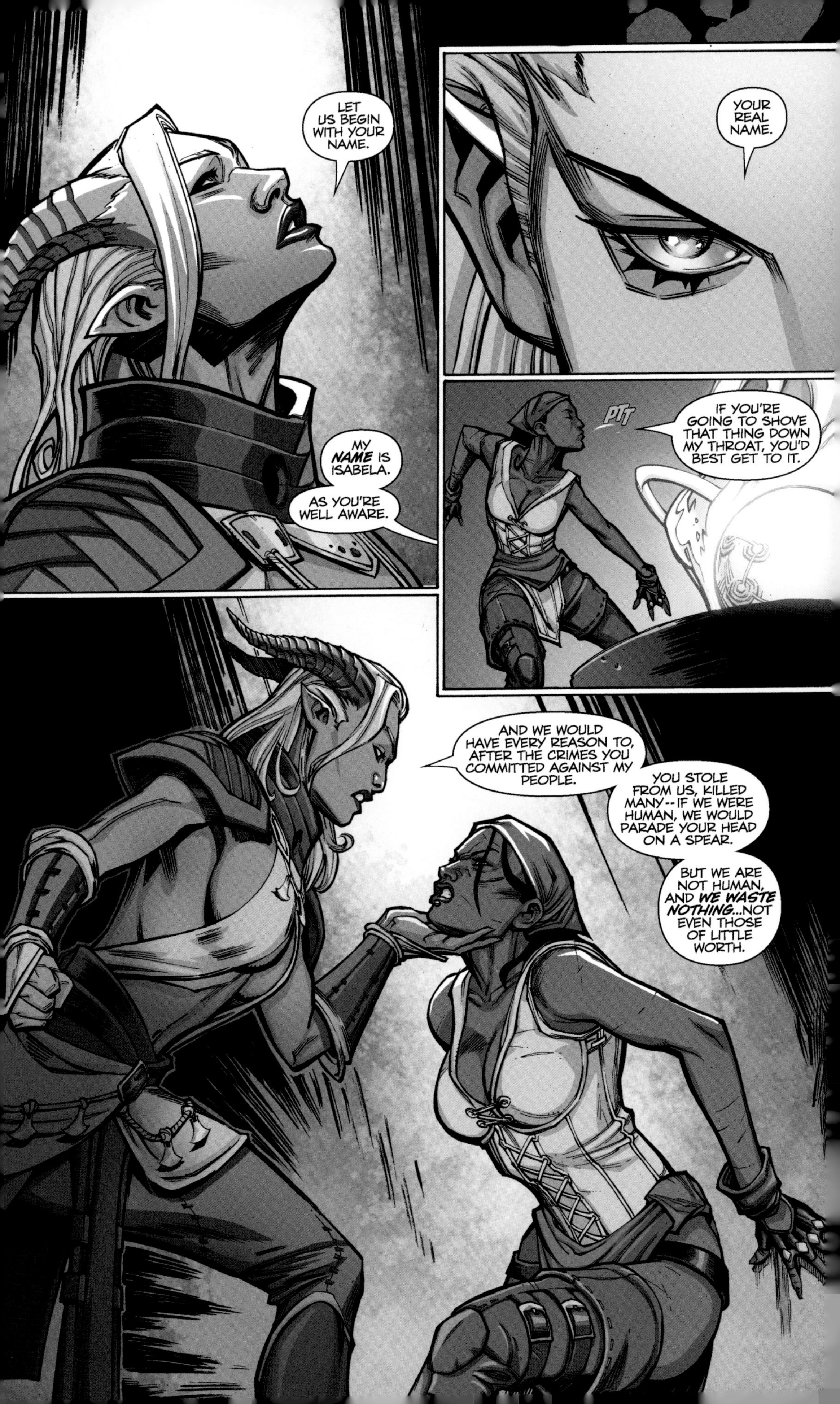
LET US BEGIN WITH YOUR NAME.
MY NAME IS ISABELA.
AS YOU'RE WELL AWARE.
YOUR REAL NAME.
PTT
IF YOU'RE GOING TO SHOVE THAT THING DOWN MY THROAT, YOU'D BEST GET TO IT.
AND WE WOULD HAVE EVERY REASON TO, AFTER THE CRIMES YOU COMMITTED AGAINST MY PEOPLE.
YOU STOLE FROM US, KILLED MANY-- IF WE WERE HUMAN, WE WOULD PARADE YOUR HEAD ON A SPEAR.
BUT WE ARE NOT HUMAN, AND WE WASTE NOTHING...NOT EVEN THOSE OF LITTLE WORTH.

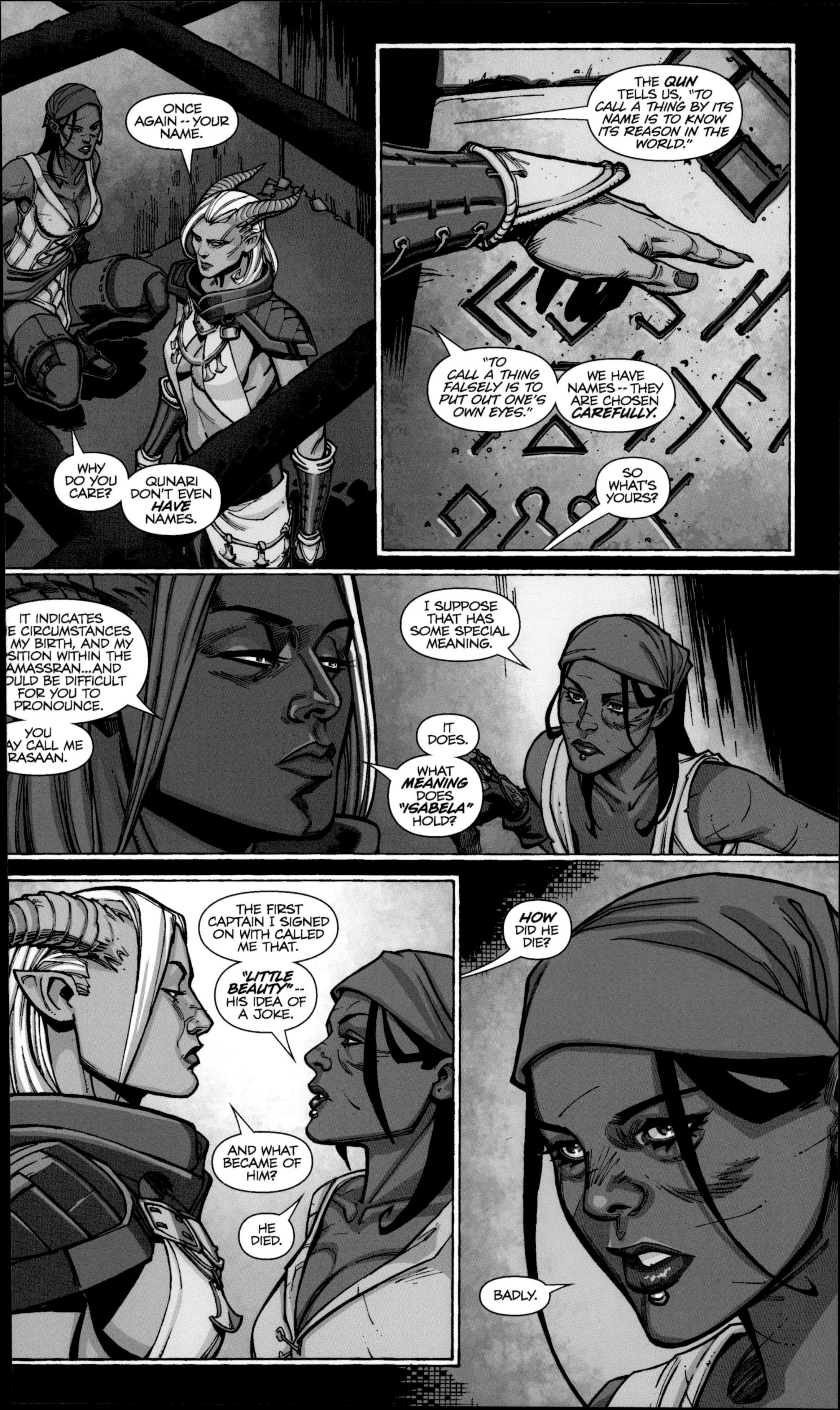

ONCE AGAIN -- YOUR NAME.
WHY DO YOU CARE?
QUNARI DON'T EVEN HAVE NAMES.
THE QUN TELLS US, "TO CALL A THING BY ITS NAME IS TO KNOW ITS REASON IN THE WORLD."
"TO CALL A THING FALSELY IS TO PUT OUT ONE'S OWN EYES."
WE HAVE NAMES -- THEY ARE CHOSEN CAREFULLY.
SO WHAT'S YOURS?
IT INDICATES E CIRCUMSTANCES MY BIRTH, AND MY SITION WITHIN THE AMASSRAN...AND OULD BE DIFFICULT FOR YOU TO PRONOUNCE.
YOU AY CALL ME RASAAN.
I SUPPOSE THAT HAS SOME SPECIAL MEANING.
IT DOES.
WHAT MEANING DOES "ISABELA" HOLD?
THE FIRST CAPTAIN I SIGNED ON WITH CALLED ME THAT.
"LITTLE BEAUTY" -- HIS IDEA OF A JOKE.
AND WHAT BECAME OF HIM?
HE DIED.
HOW DID HE DIE?
BADLY.

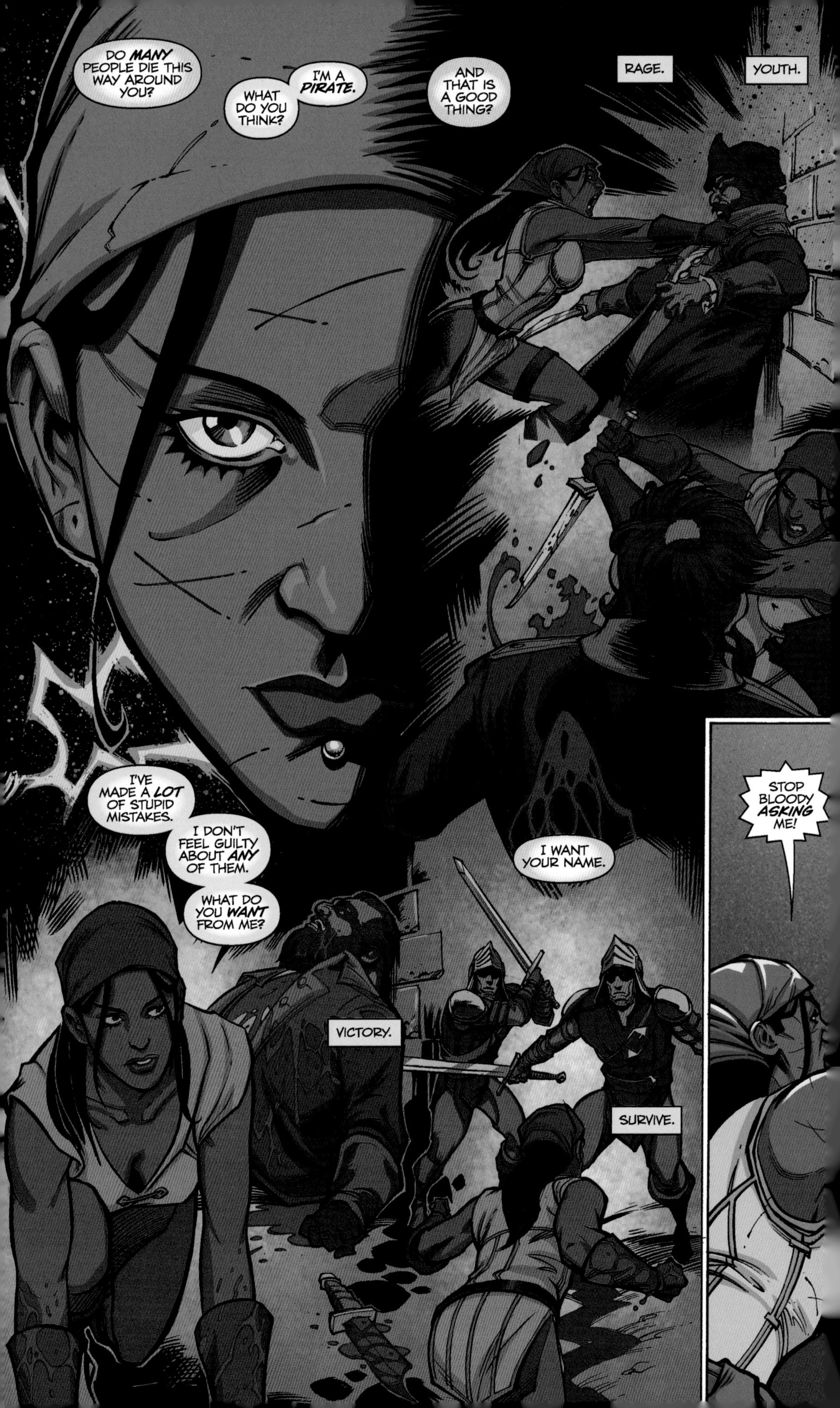
DO MANY PEOPLE DIE THIS WAY AROUND YOU?
WHAT DO YOU THINK?
I'M A PIRATE.
AND THAT IS A GOOD THING?
RAGE.
YOUTH.
I'VE MADE A LOT OF STUPID MISTAKES.
I DON'T FEEL GUILTY ABOUT ANY OF THEM.
WHAT DO YOU WANT FROM ME?
I WANT YOUR NAME.
VICTORY.
SURVIVE.
STOP BLOODY ASKING ME!

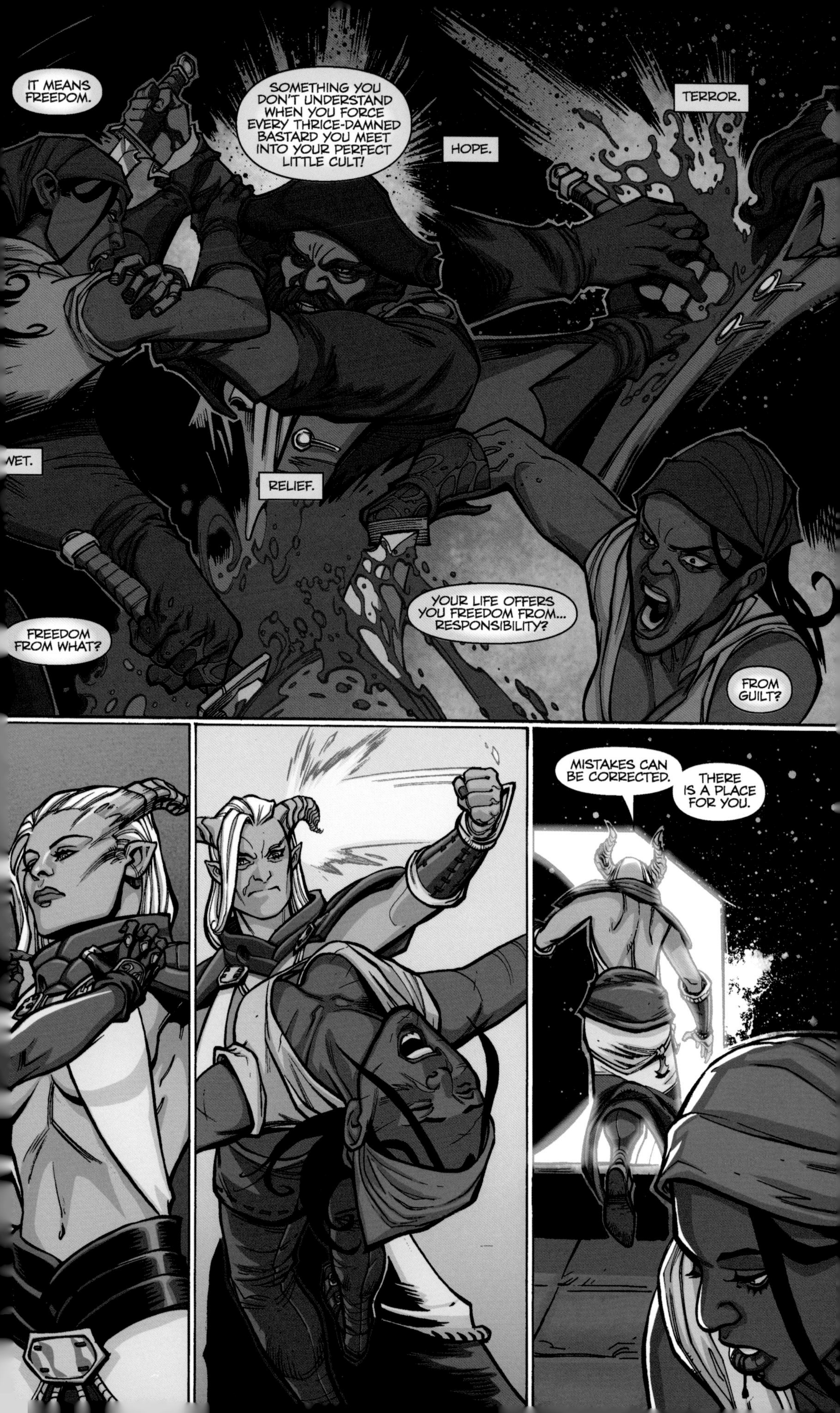
IT MEANS FREEDOM.
SOMETHING YOU DON'T UNDERSTAND WHEN YOU FORCE EVERY THRICE-DAMNED BASTARD YOU MEET INTO YOUR PERFECT LITTLE CULT!
HOPE.
TERROR.
WET.
RELIEF.
YOUR LIFE OFFERS YOU FREEDOM FROM... RESPONSIBILITY?
FREEDOM FROM WHAT?
FROM GUILT?
MISTAKES CAN BE CORRECTED.
THERE IS A PLACE FOR YOU.

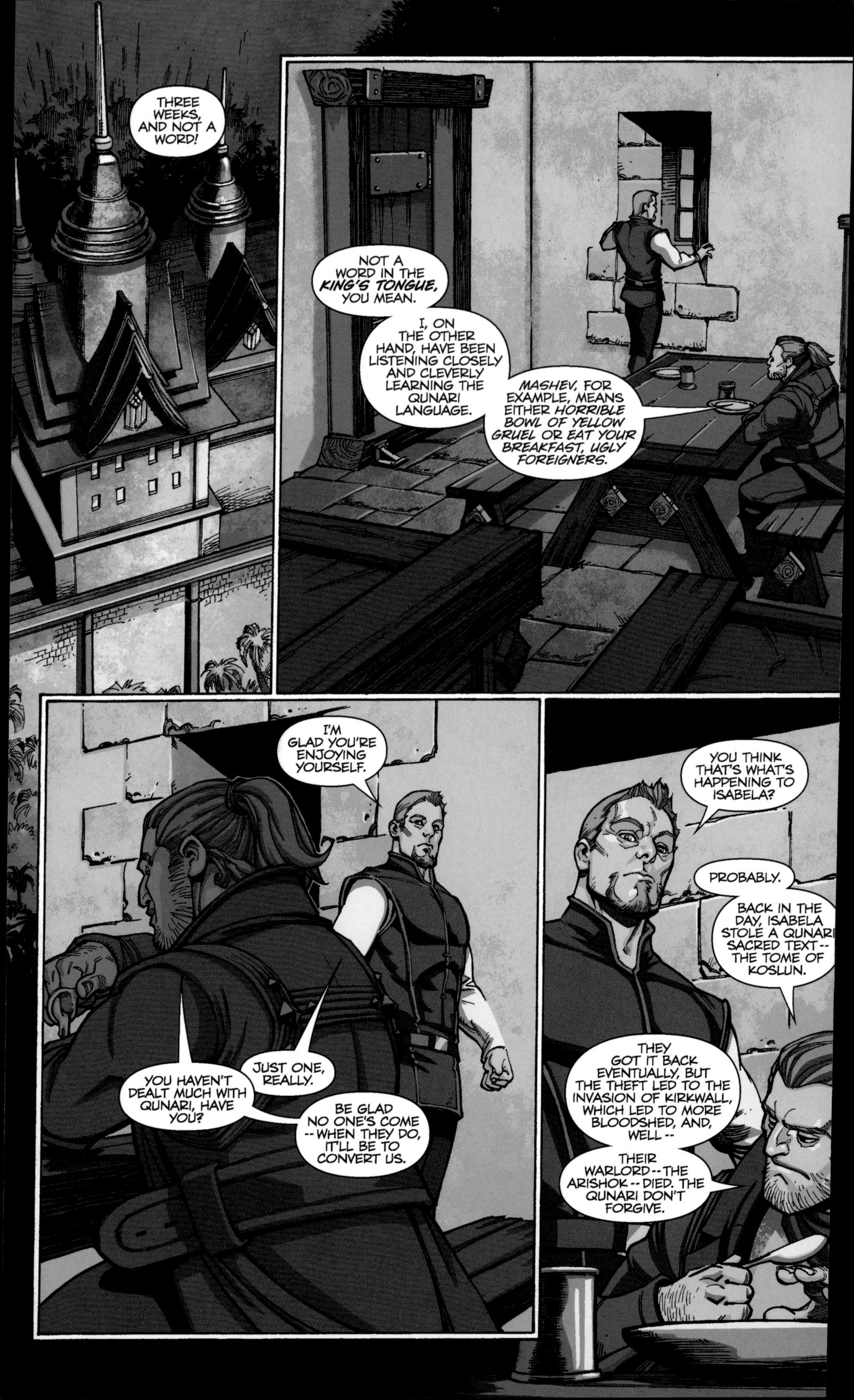
THREE WEEKS, AND NOT A WORD!
NOT A WORD IN THE KING'S TONGUE, YOU MEAN.
I, ON THE OTHER HAND, HAVE BEEN LISTENING CLOSELY AND CLEVERLY LEARNING THE QUNARI LANGUAGE.
MASHEV, FOR EXAMPLE, MEANS EITHER HORRIBLE BOWL OF YELLOW GRUEL OR EAT YOUR BREAKFAST, UGLY FOREIGNERS.
I'M GLAD YOU'RE ENJOYING YOURSELF.
YOU HAVEN'T DEALT MUCH WITH QUNARI, HAVE YOU?
JUST ONE, REALLY.
BE GLAD NO ONE'S COME -- WHEN THEY DO, IT'LL BE TO CONVERT US.
YOU THINK THAT'S WHAT'S HAPPENING TO ISABELA?
PROBABLY.
BACK IN THE DAY, ISABELA STOLE A QUNARI SACRED TEXT -- THE TOME OF KOSLUN.
THEY GOT IT BACK EVENTUALLY, BUT THE THEFT LED TO THE INVASION OF KIRKWALL, WHICH LED TO MORE BLOODSHED, AND, WELL --
THEIR WARLORD -- THE ARISHOK -- DIED. THE QUNARI DON'T FORGIVE.

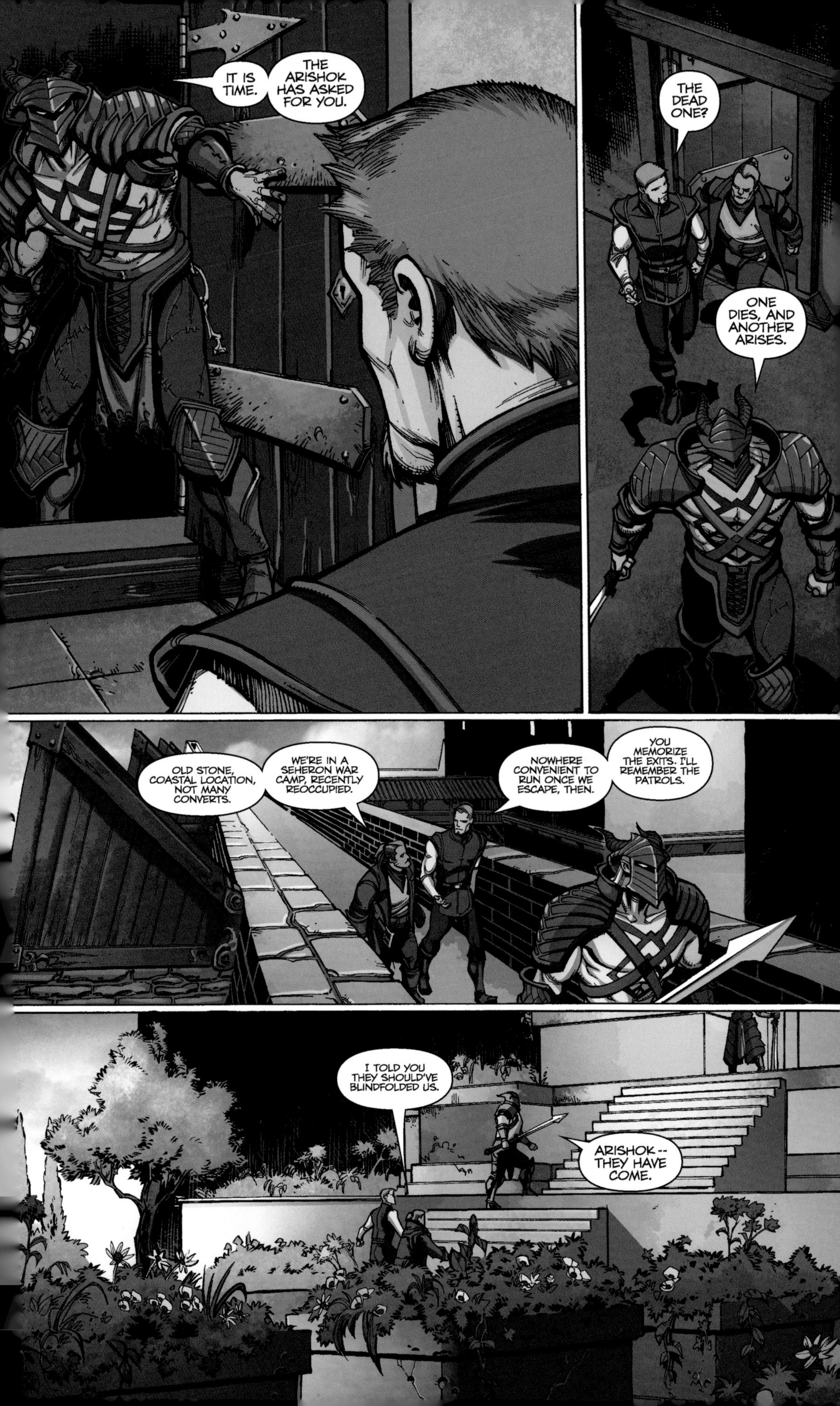

IT IS TIME.
THE ARISHOK HAS ASKED FOR YOU.
THE DEAD ONE?
ONE DIES, AND ANOTHER ARISES.
OLD STONE, COASTAL LOCATION, NOT MANY CONVERTS.
WE'RE IN A SEHERON WAR CAMP, RECENTLY REOCCUPIED.
NOWHERE CONVENIENT TO RUN ONCE WE ESCAPE, THEN.
YOU MEMORIZE THE EXITS. I'LL REMEMBER THE PATROLS.
I TOLD YOU THEY SHOULD'VE BLINDFOLDED US.
ARISHOK -- THEY HAVE COME.

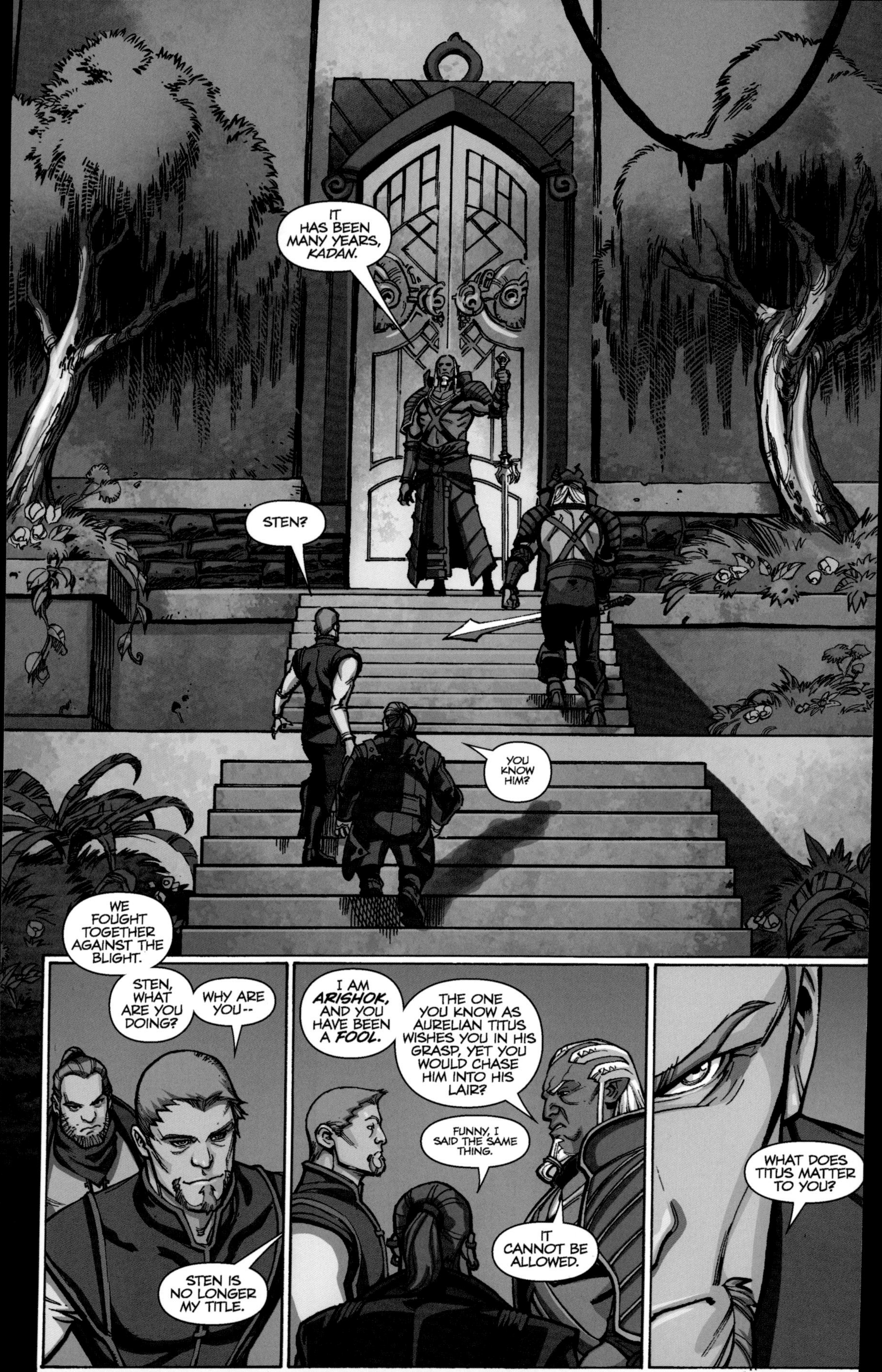
IT HAS BEEN MANY YEARS, *KADAN.*
STEN?
YOU KNOW HIM?
WE FOUGHT TOGETHER AGAINST THE BLIGHT.
STEN, WHAT ARE YOU DOING?
WHY ARE YOU--
STEN IS NO LONGER MY TITLE.
I AM ***ARISHOK,*** AND YOU HAVE BEEN A ***FOOL.***
THE ONE YOU KNOW AS AURELIAN TITUS WISHES YOU IN HIS GRASP, YET YOU WOULD CHASE HIM INTO HIS LAIR?
FUNNY, I SAID THE SAME THING.
IT CANNOT BE ALLOWED.
WHAT DOES TITUS MATTER TO YOU?

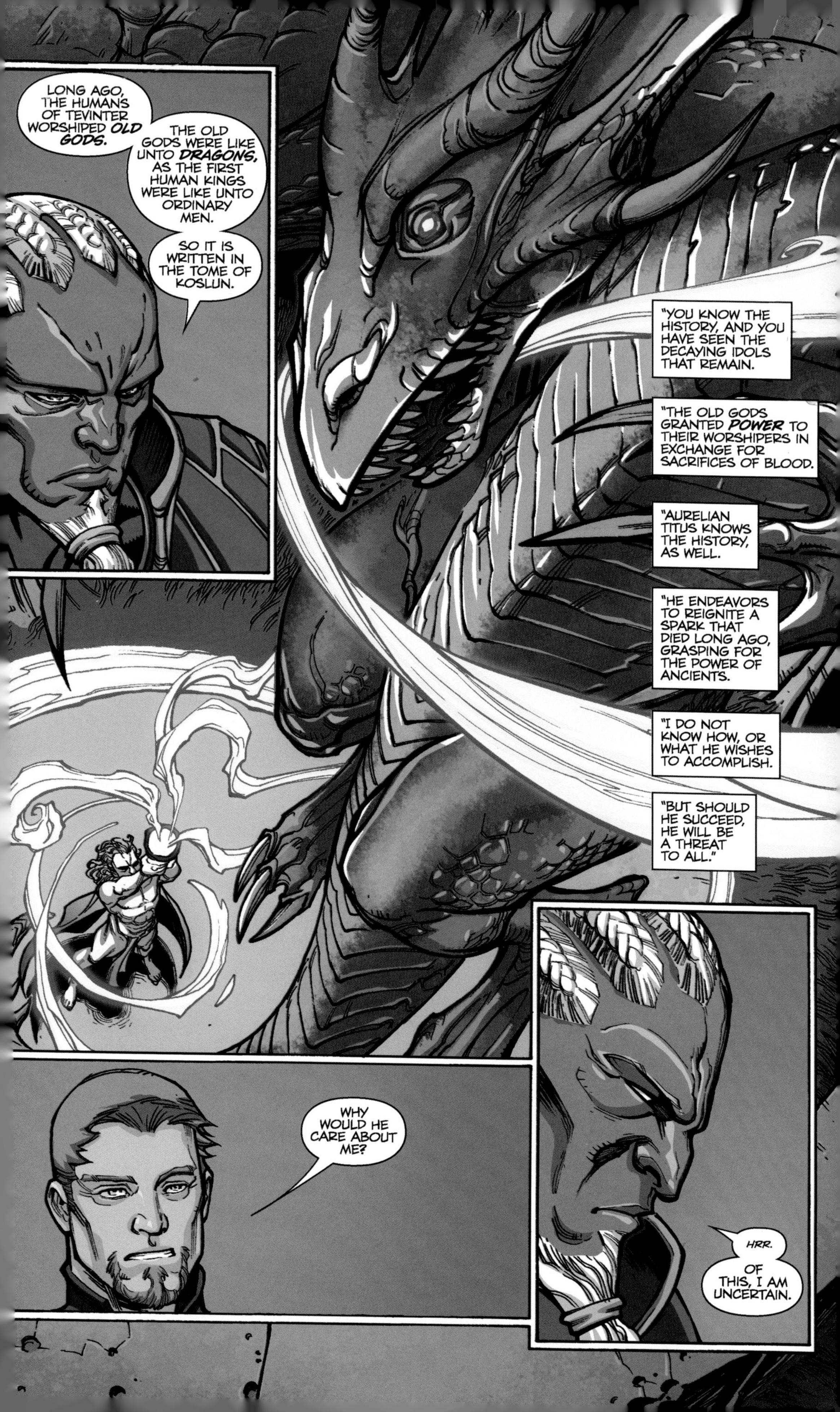
LONG AGO, THE HUMANS OF TEVINTER WORSHIPED **OLD GODS.**
THE OLD GODS WERE LIKE UNTO **DRAGONS,** AS THE FIRST HUMAN KINGS WERE LIKE UNTO ORDINARY MEN.
SO IT IS WRITTEN IN THE TOME OF KOSLUN.
"YOU KNOW THE HISTORY, AND YOU HAVE SEEN THE DECAYING IDOLS THAT REMAIN.
"THE OLD GODS GRANTED **POWER** TO THEIR WORSHIPERS IN EXCHANGE FOR SACRIFICES OF BLOOD.
"AURELIAN TITUS KNOWS THE HISTORY, AS WELL.
"HE ENDEAVORS TO REIGNITE A SPARK THAT DIED LONG AGO, GRASPING FOR THE POWER OF ANCIENTS.
"I DO NOT KNOW HOW, OR WHAT HE WISHES TO ACCOMPLISH.
"BUT SHOULD HE SUCCEED, HE WILL BE A THREAT TO ALL."
WHY WOULD HE CARE ABOUT ME?
HRR.
OF THIS, I AM UNCERTAIN.

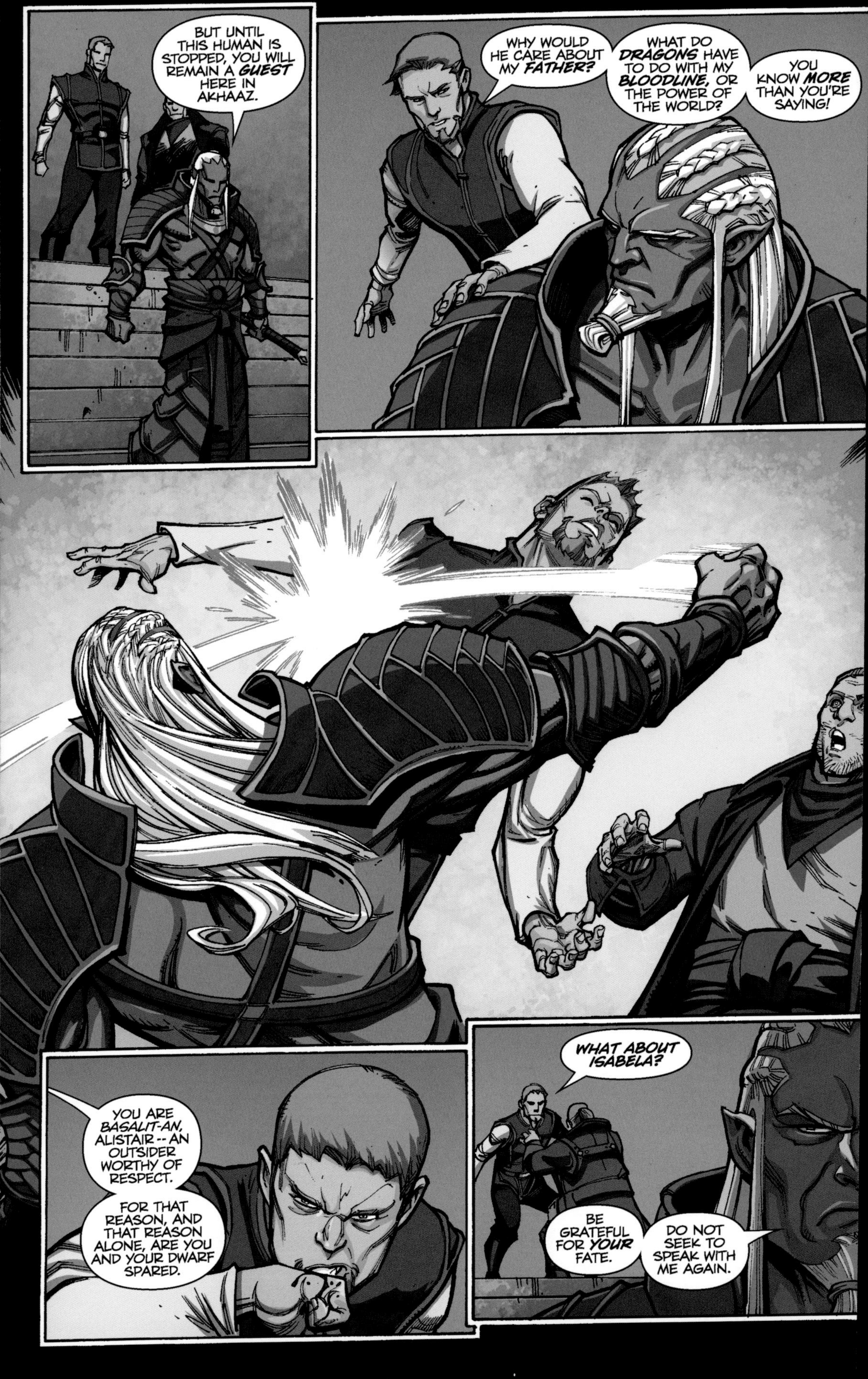

BUT UNTIL THIS HUMAN IS STOPPED, YOU WILL REMAIN A *GUEST* HERE IN AKHAAZ.
WHY WOULD HE CARE ABOUT MY *FATHER?*
WHAT DO *DRAGONS* HAVE TO DO WITH MY *BLOODLINE,* OR THE POWER OF THE WORLD?
YOU KNOW *MORE* THAN YOU'RE SAYING!
YOU ARE *BASALIT-AN,* ALISTAIR -- AN OUTSIDER WORTHY OF RESPECT.
FOR THAT REASON, AND THAT REASON ALONE, ARE YOU AND YOUR DWARF SPARED.
WHAT ABOUT ISABELA?
BE GRATEFUL FOR *YOUR* FATE.
DO NOT SEEK TO SPEAK WITH ME AGAIN.

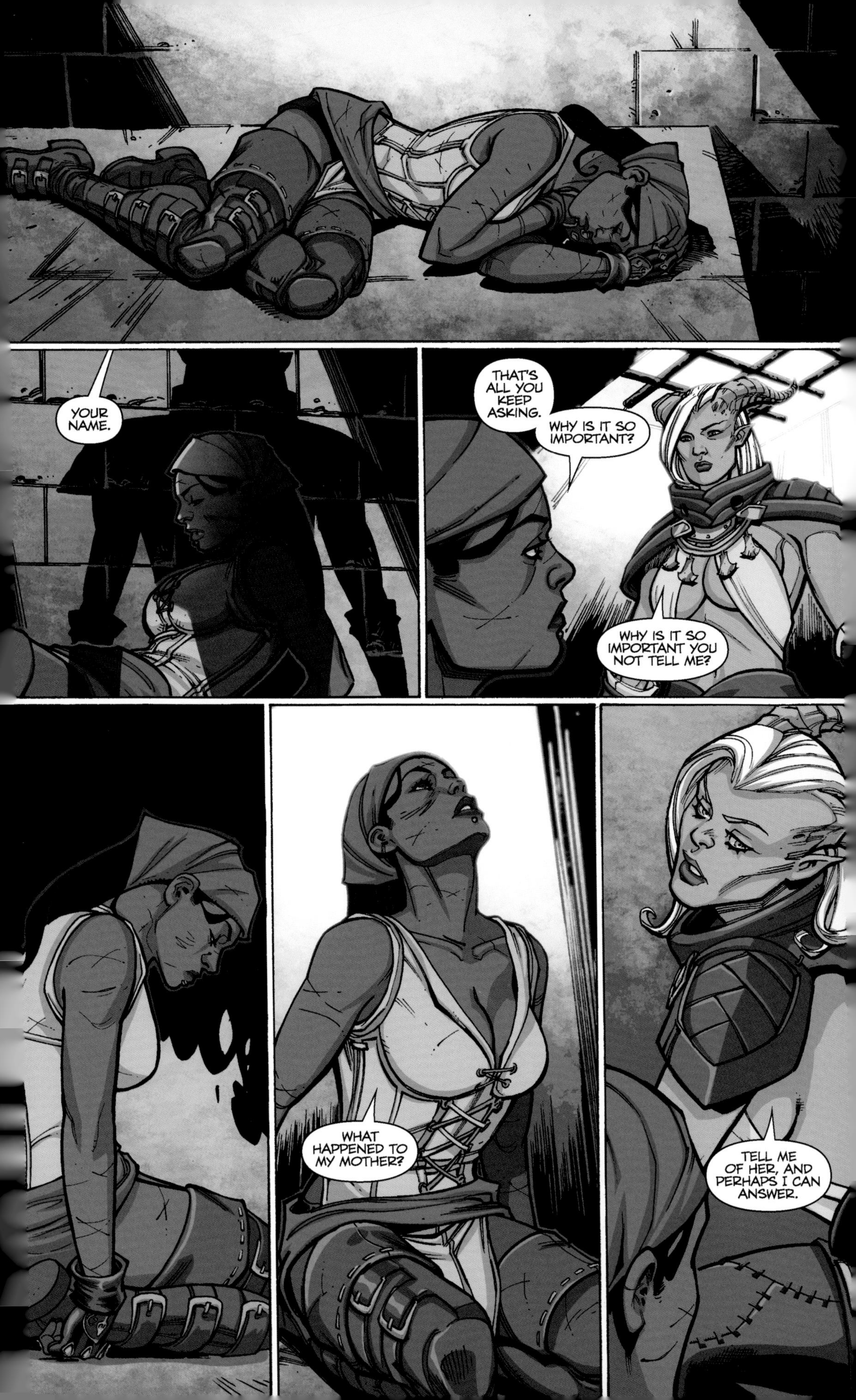
YOUR NAME.
THAT'S ALL YOU KEEP ASKING.
WHY IS IT SO IMPORTANT?
WHY IS IT SO IMPORTANT YOU NOT TELL ME?
WHAT HAPPENED TO MY MOTHER?
TELL ME OF HER, AND PERHAPS I CAN ANSWER.

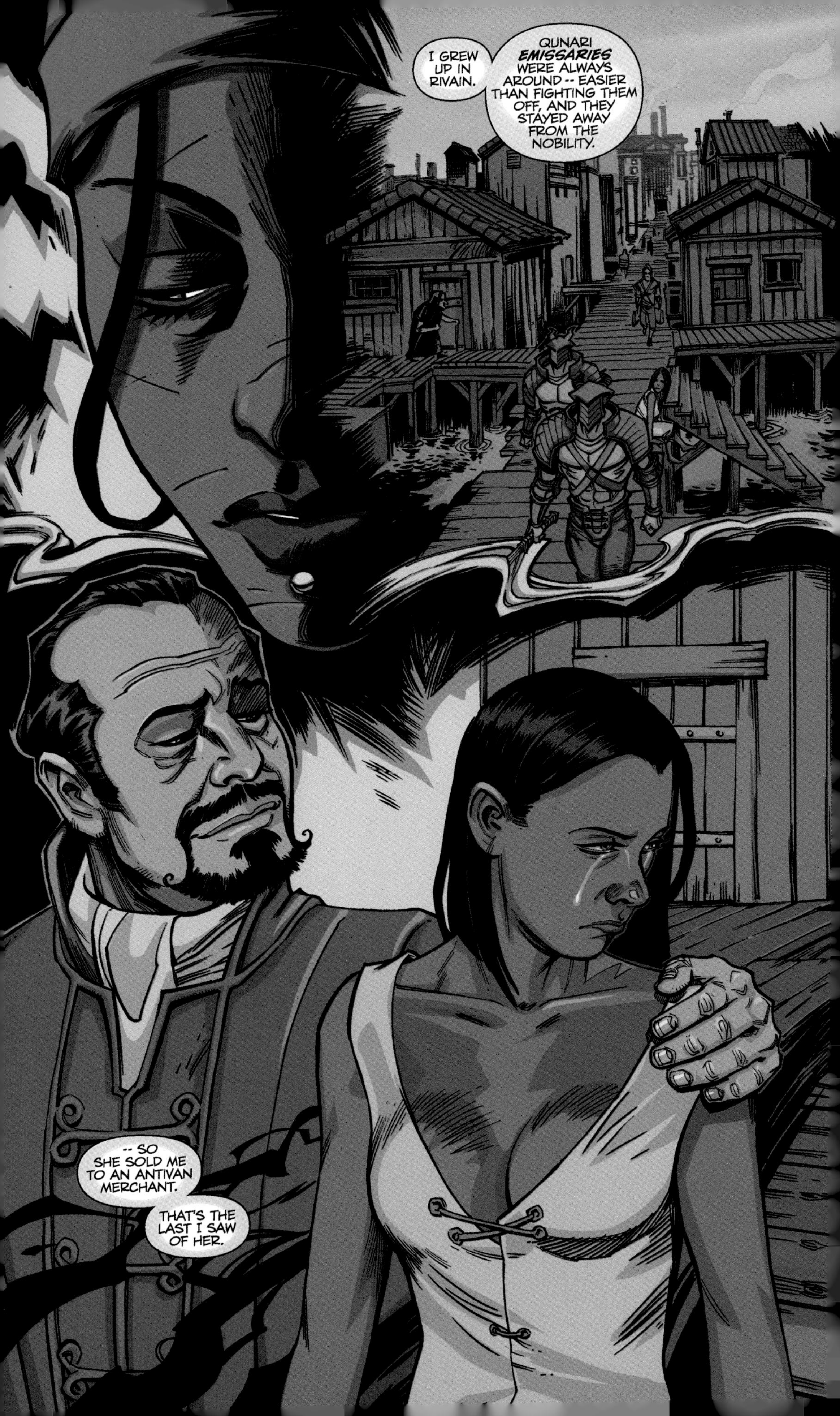
I GREW UP IN RIVAIN.
QUNARI EMISSARIES WERE ALWAYS AROUND -- EASIER THAN FIGHTING THEM OFF, AND THEY STAYED AWAY FROM THE NOBILITY.
-- SO SHE SOLD ME TO AN ANTIVAN MERCHANT.
THAT'S THE LAST I SAW OF HER.

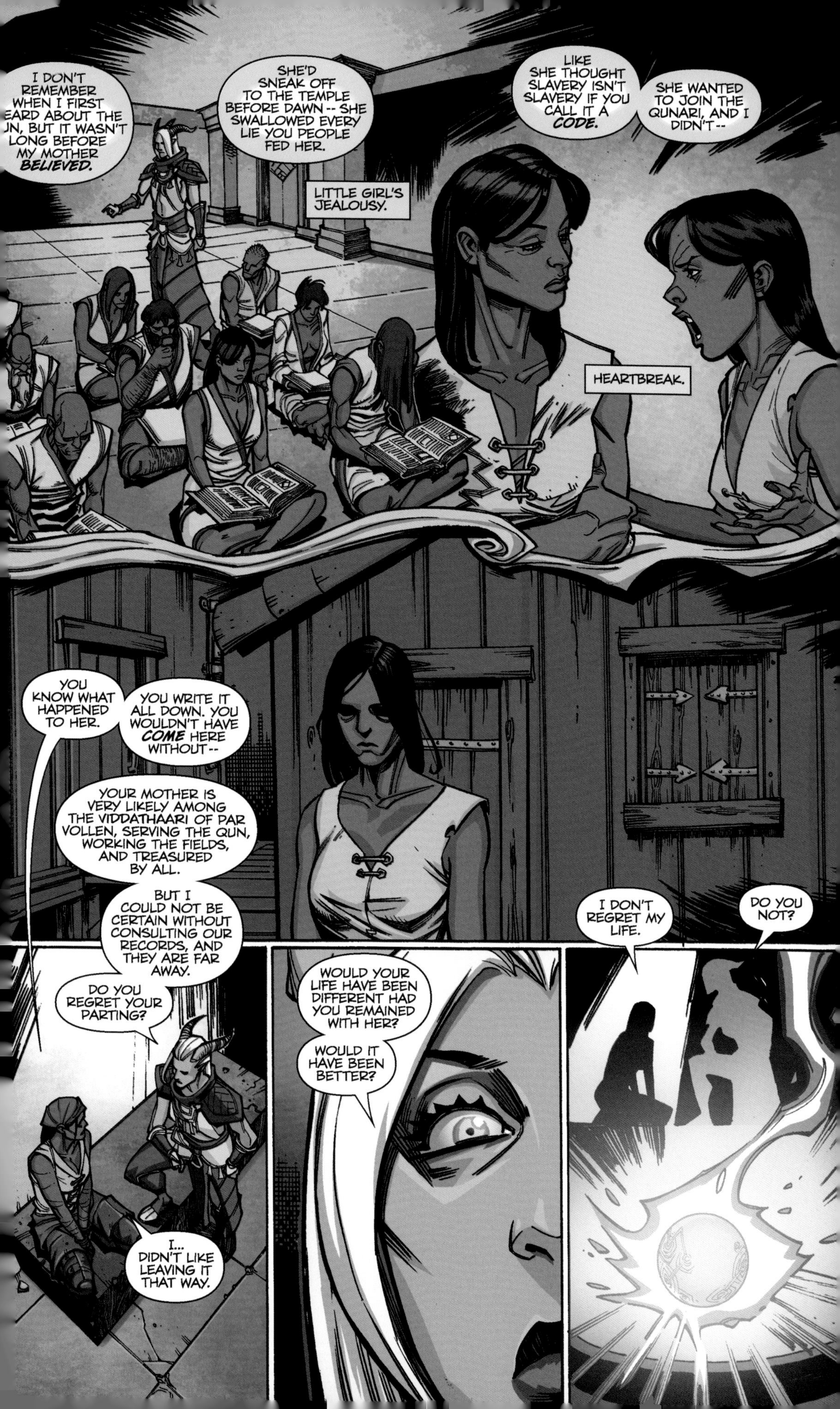

I DON'T REMEMBER WHEN I FIRST EARD ABOUT THE UN, BUT IT WASN'T LONG BEFORE MY MOTHER BELIEVED.
SHE'D SNEAK OFF TO THE TEMPLE BEFORE DAWN -- SHE SWALLOWED EVERY LIE YOU PEOPLE FED HER.
LITTLE GIRL'S JEALOUSY.
LIKE SHE THOUGHT SLAVERY ISN'T SLAVERY IF YOU CALL IT A CODE.
SHE WANTED TO JOIN THE QUNARI, AND I DIDN'T --
HEARTBREAK.
YOU KNOW WHAT HAPPENED TO HER.
YOU WRITE IT ALL DOWN. YOU WOULDN'T HAVE COME HERE WITHOUT --
YOUR MOTHER IS VERY LIKELY AMONG THE VIDDATHAARI OF PAR VOLLEN, SERVING THE QUN, WORKING THE FIELDS, AND TREASURED BY ALL.
BUT I COULD NOT BE CERTAIN WITHOUT CONSULTING OUR RECORDS, AND THEY ARE FAR AWAY.
DO YOU REGRET YOUR PARTING?
I... DIDN'T LIKE LEAVING IT THAT WAY.
WOULD YOUR LIFE HAVE BEEN DIFFERENT HAD YOU REMAINED WITH HER?
WOULD IT HAVE BEEN BETTER?
I DON'T REGRET MY LIFE.
DO YOU NOT?

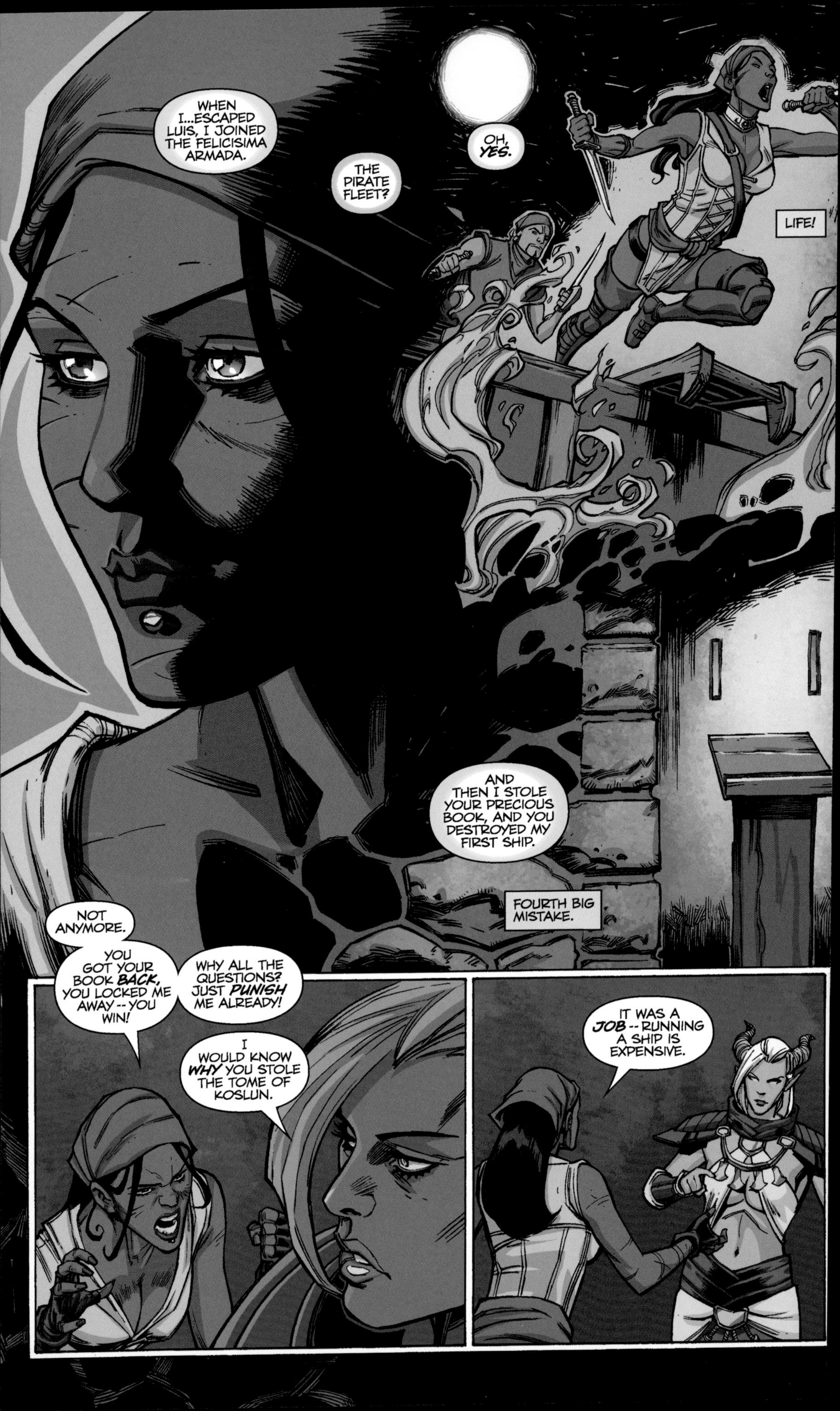
WHEN I...ESCAPED LUIS, I JOINED THE FELICISIMA ARMADA.
THE PIRATE FLEET?
OH, YES.
LIFE!
AND THEN I STOLE YOUR PRECIOUS BOOK, AND YOU DESTROYED MY FIRST SHIP.
FOURTH BIG MISTAKE.
NOT ANYMORE.
YOU GOT YOUR BOOK BACK, YOU LOCKED ME AWAY -- YOU WIN!
WHY ALL THE QUESTIONS? JUST PUNISH ME ALREADY!
I WOULD KNOW WHY YOU STOLE THE TOME OF KOSLUN.
IT WAS A JOB -- RUNNING A SHIP IS EXPENSIVE.

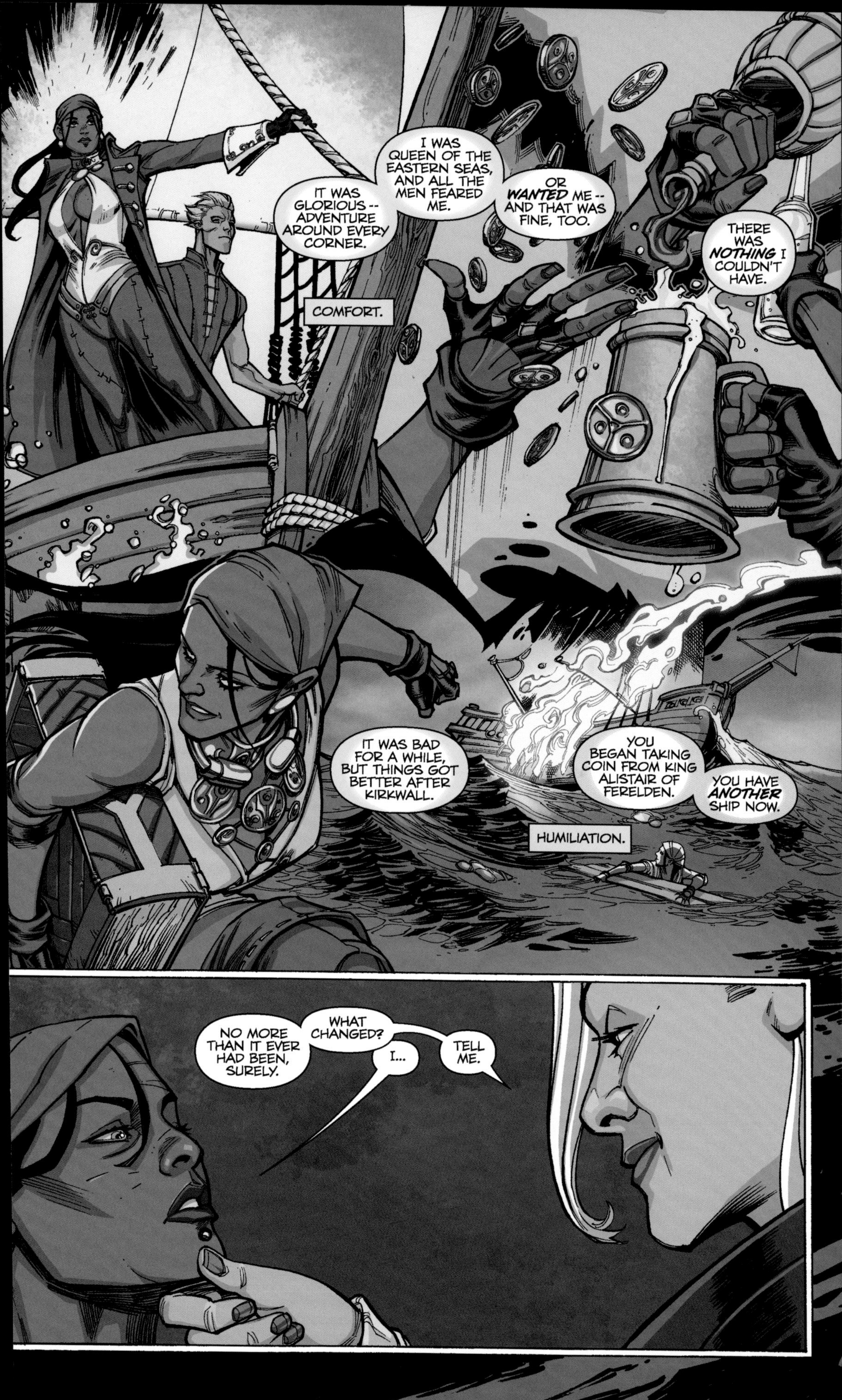

IT WAS GLORIOUS -- ADVENTURE AROUND EVERY CORNER.
I WAS QUEEN OF THE EASTERN SEAS, AND ALL THE MEN FEARED ME.
OR *WANTED* ME -- AND THAT WAS FINE, TOO.
COMFORT.
THERE WAS *NOTHING* I COULDN'T HAVE.
IT WAS BAD FOR A WHILE, BUT THINGS GOT BETTER AFTER KIRKWALL.
YOU BEGAN TAKING COIN FROM KING ALISTAIR OF FERELDEN.
YOU HAVE *ANOTHER* SHIP NOW.
HUMILIATION.
NO MORE THAN IT EVER HAD BEEN, SURELY.
WHAT CHANGED?
I...
TELL ME.

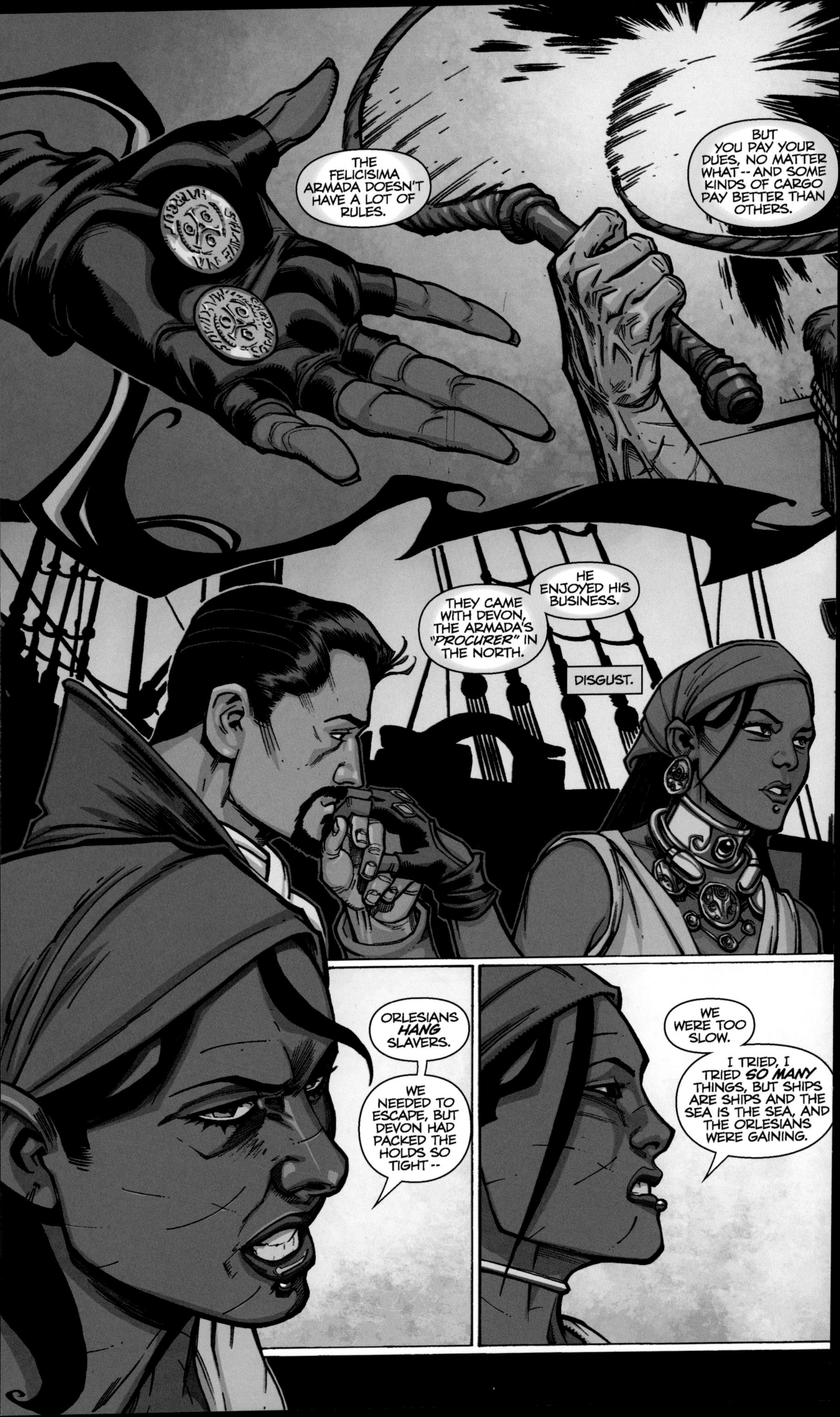
THE FELICISIMA ARMADA DOESN'T HAVE A LOT OF RULES.
BUT YOU PAY YOUR DUES, NO MATTER WHAT -- AND SOME KINDS OF CARGO PAY BETTER THAN OTHERS.
THEY CAME WITH DEVON, THE ARMADA'S "PROCURER" IN THE NORTH.
HE ENJOYED HIS BUSINESS.
DISGUST.
ORLESIANS HANG SLAVERS.
WE NEEDED TO ESCAPE, BUT DEVON HAD PACKED THE HOLDS SO TIGHT --
WE WERE TOO SLOW.
I TRIED, I TRIED SO MANY THINGS, BUT SHIPS ARE SHIPS AND THE SEA IS THE SEA, AND THE ORLESIANS WERE GAINING.

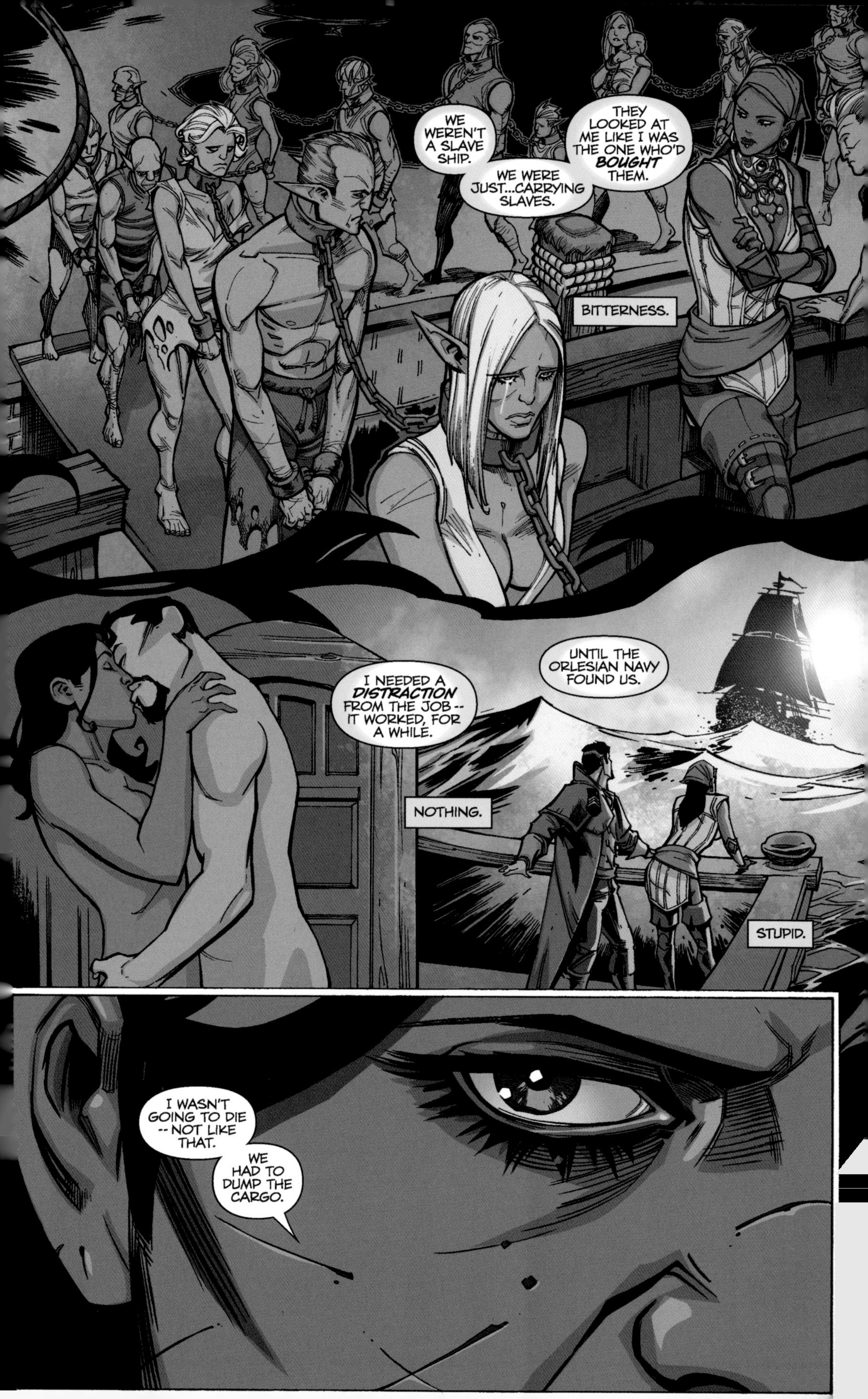
WE WEREN'T A SLAVE SHIP.
WE WERE JUST...CARRYING SLAVES.
THEY LOOKED AT ME LIKE I WAS THE ONE WHO'D BOUGHT THEM.
BITTERNESS.
I NEEDED A DISTRACTION FROM THE JOB -- IT WORKED, FOR A WHILE.
NOTHING.
UNTIL THE ORLESIAN NAVY FOUND US.
STUPID.
I WASN'T GOING TO DIE -- NOT LIKE THAT.
WE HAD TO DUMP THE CARGO.

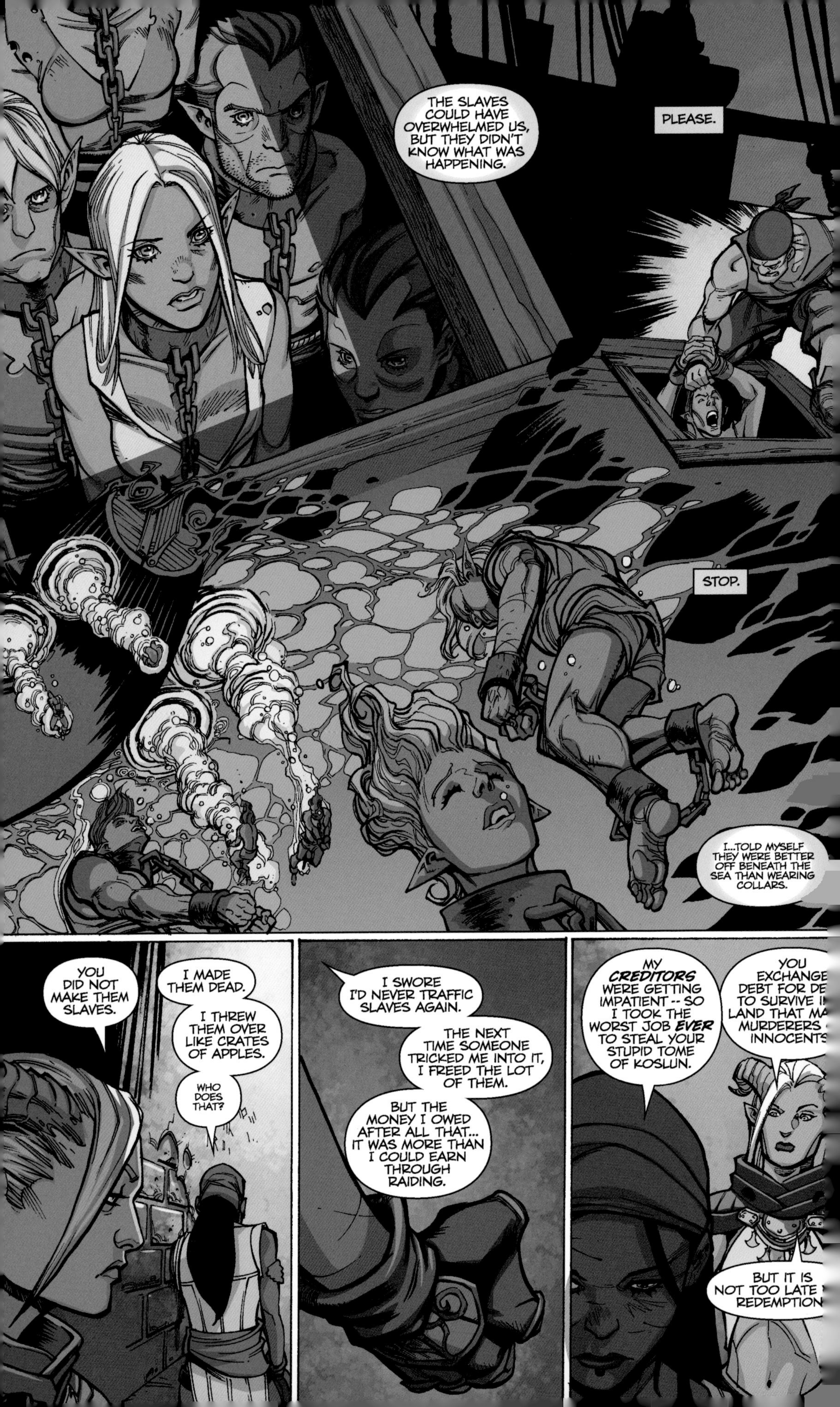
THE SLAVES COULD HAVE OVERWHELMED US, BUT THEY DIDN'T KNOW WHAT WAS HAPPENING.
PLEASE.
STOP.
I...TOLD MYSELF THEY WERE BETTER OFF BENEATH THE SEA THAN WEARING COLLARS.
YOU DID NOT MAKE THEM SLAVES.
I MADE THEM DEAD.
I THREW THEM OVER LIKE CRATES OF APPLES.
WHO DOES THAT?
I SWORE I'D NEVER TRAFFIC SLAVES AGAIN.
THE NEXT TIME SOMEONE TRICKED ME INTO IT, I FREED THE LOT OF THEM.
BUT THE MONEY I OWED AFTER ALL THAT... IT WAS MORE THAN I COULD EARN THROUGH RAIDING.
MY CREDITORS WERE GETTING IMPATIENT -- SO I TOOK THE WORST JOB EVER TO STEAL YOUR STUPID TOME OF KOSLUN.
BUT IT IS NOT TOO LATE

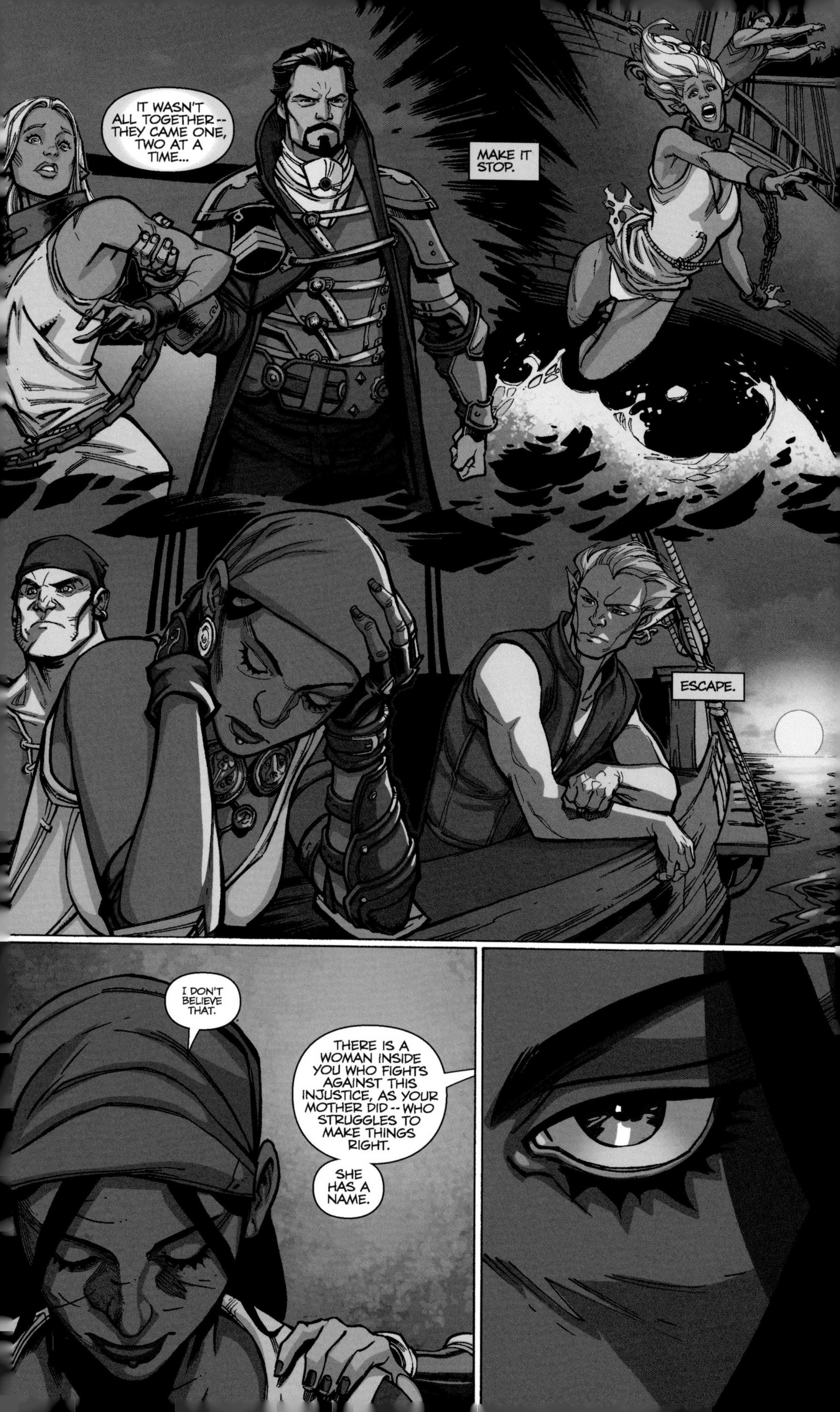
IT WASN'T ALL TOGETHER -- THEY CAME ONE, TWO AT A TIME...
MAKE IT STOP.
ESCAPE.
I DON'T BELIEVE THAT.
THERE IS A WOMAN INSIDE YOU WHO FIGHTS AGAINST THIS INJUSTICE, AS YOUR MOTHER DID -- WHO STRUGGLES TO MAKE THINGS RIGHT.
SHE HAS A NAME.

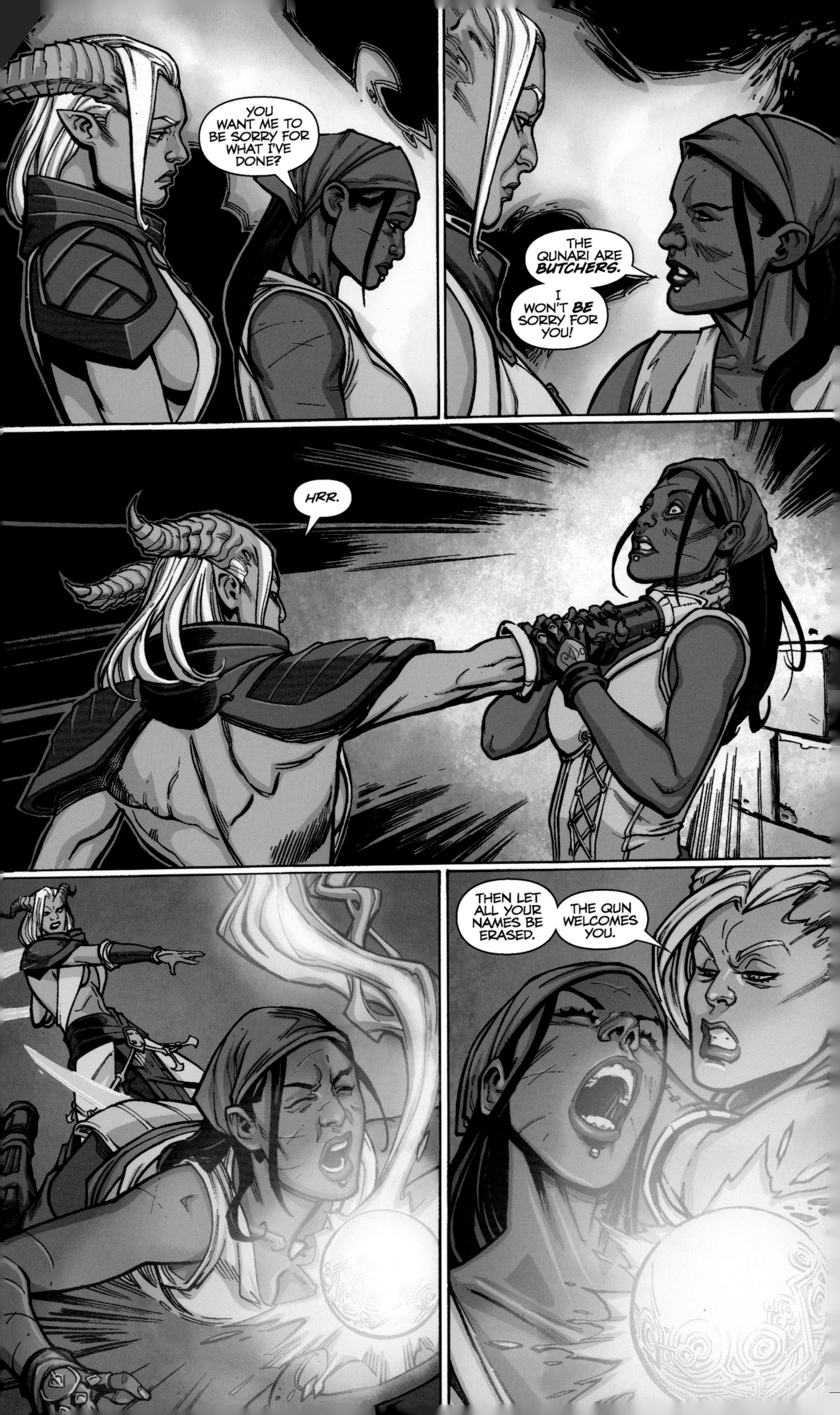
YOU WANT ME TO BE SORRY FOR WHAT I'VE DONE?
THE QUNARI ARE BUTCHERS.
I WON'T BE SORRY FOR YOU!
HRR.
THEN LET ALL YOUR NAMES BE ERASED.
THE QUN WELCOMES YOU.

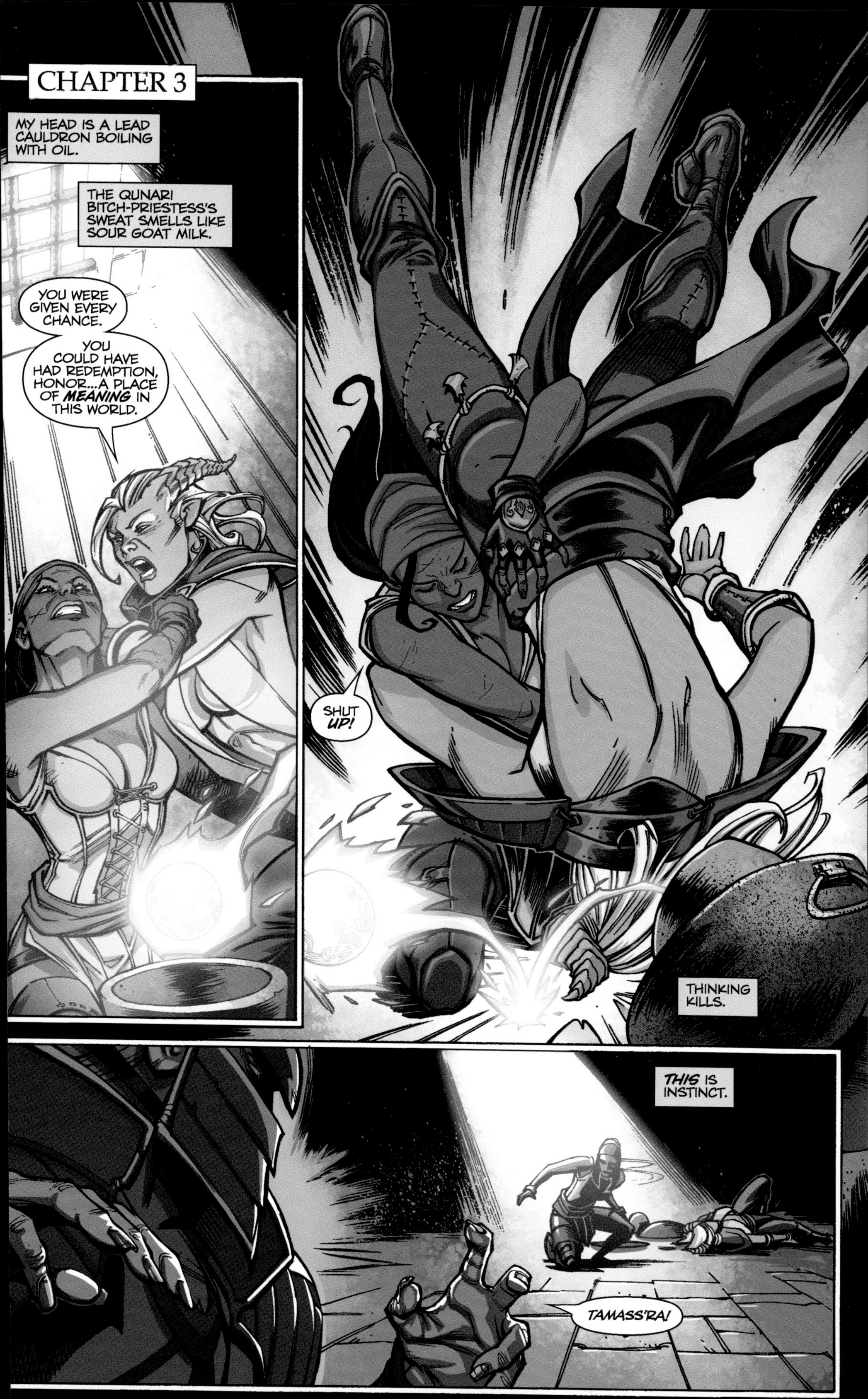
CHAPTER 3
MY HEAD IS A LEAD CAULDRON BOILING WITH OIL.
THE QUNARI BITCH-PRIESTESS'S SWEAT SMELLS LIKE SOUR GOAT MILK.
YOU WERE GIVEN EVERY CHANCE.
YOU COULD HAVE HAD REDEMPTION, HONOR...A PLACE OF MEANING IN THIS WORLD.
SHUT UP!
THINKING KILLS.
THIS IS INSTINCT.
TAMASS'RA!

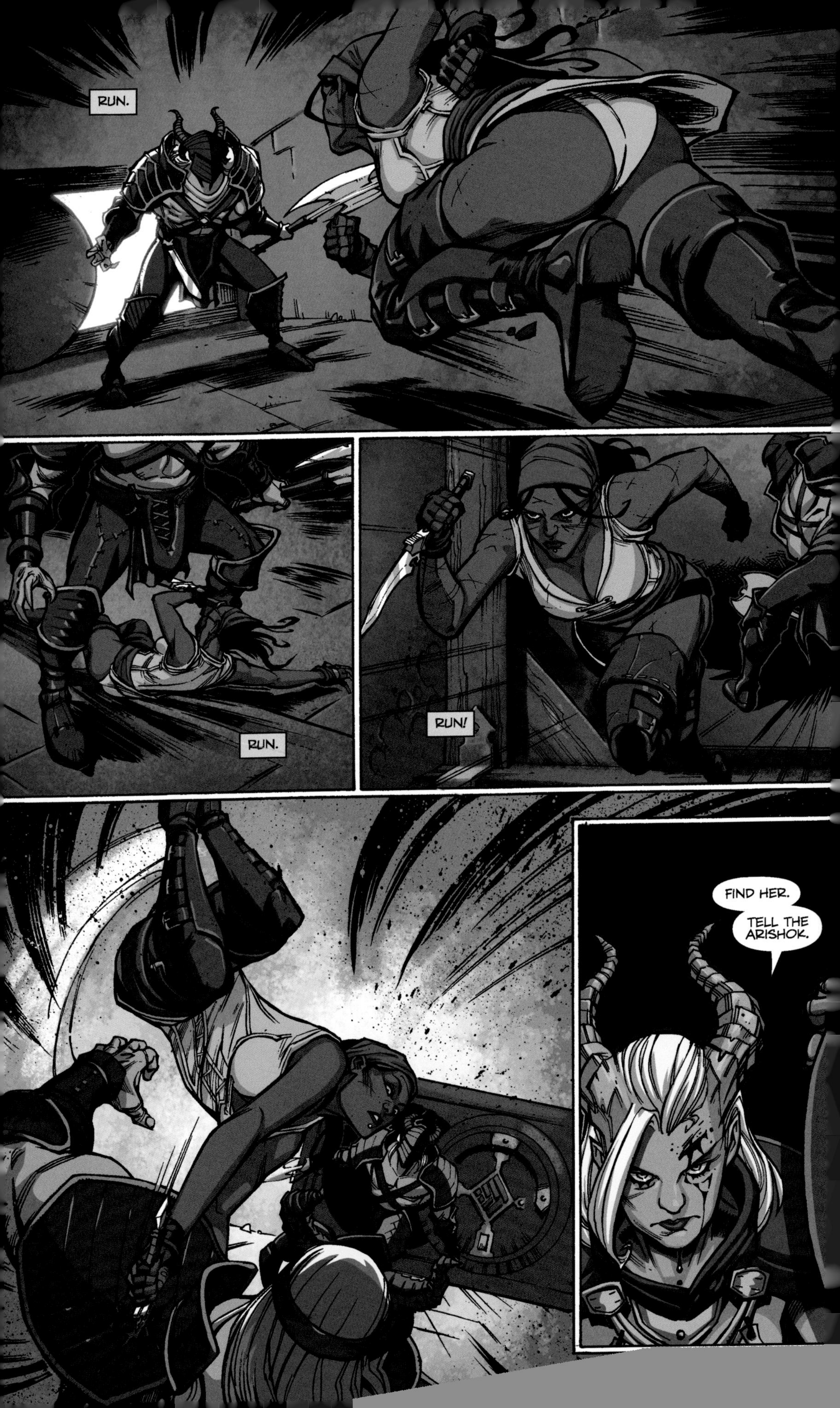

RUN.
RUN.
RUN!
FIND HER.
TELL THE ARISHOK.

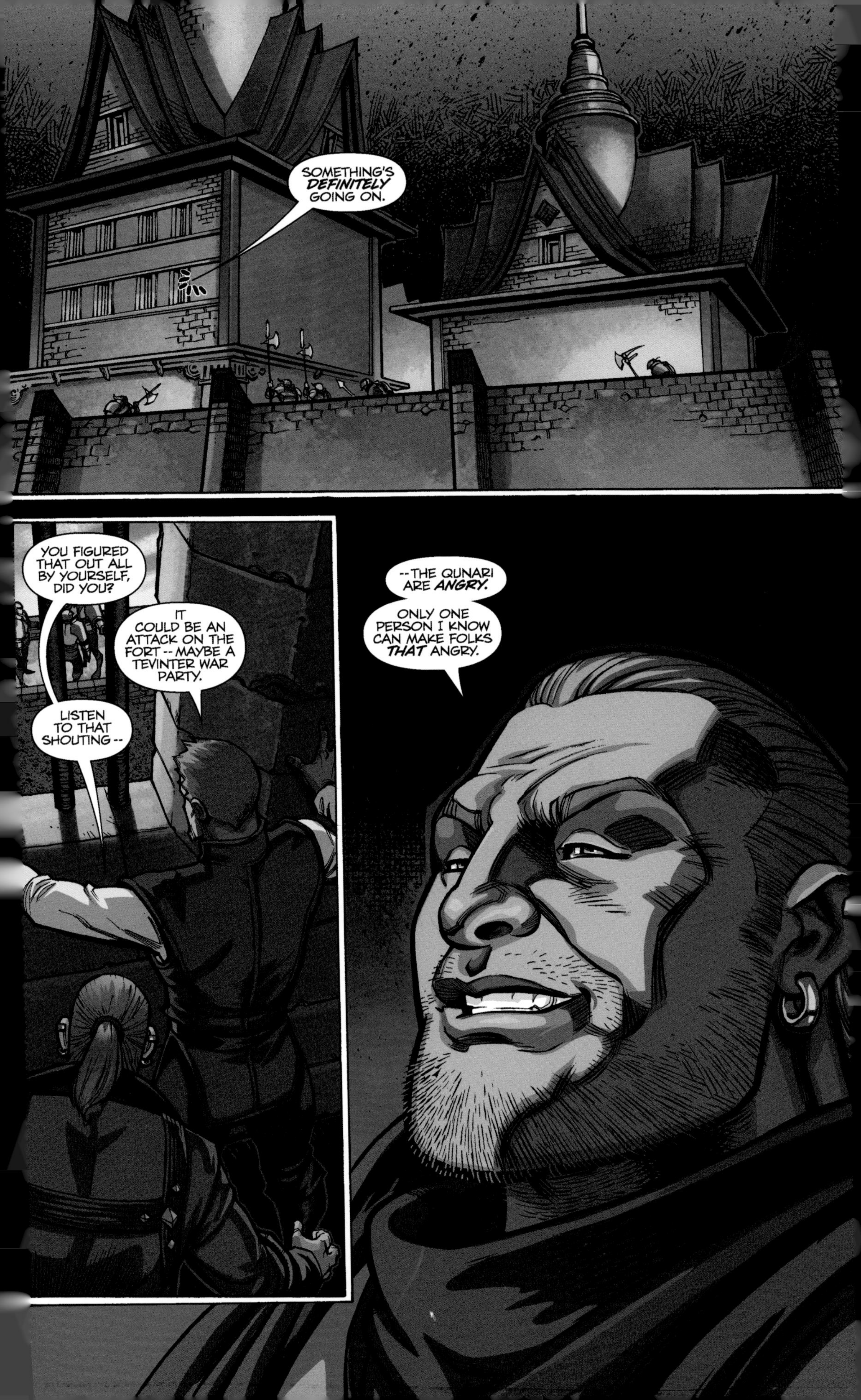
SOMETHING'S *DEFINITELY* GOING ON.
YOU FIGURED THAT OUT ALL BY YOURSELF, DID YOU?
IT COULD BE AN ATTACK ON THE FORT -- MAYBE A TEVINTER WAR PARTY.
LISTEN TO THAT SHOUTING --
--THE QUNARI ARE *ANGRY.*
ONLY ONE PERSON I KNOW CAN MAKE FOLKS *THAT* ANGRY.

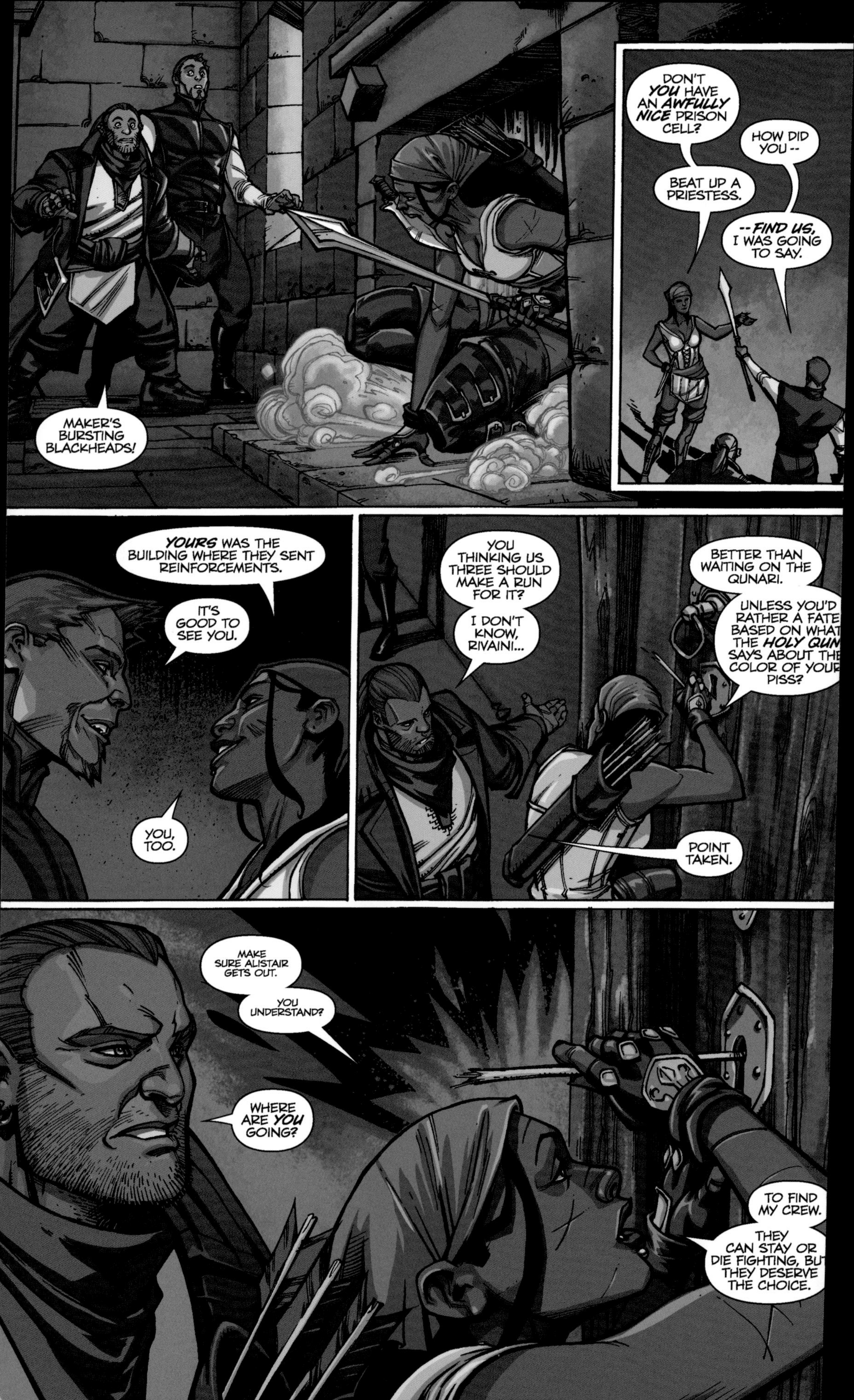
MAKER'S BURSTING BLACKHEADS!
DON'T *YOU* HAVE AN *AWFULLY NICE* PRISON CELL?
HOW DID YOU --
BEAT UP A PRIESTESS.
-- *FIND US,* I WAS GOING TO SAY.
YOURS WAS THE BUILDING WHERE THEY SENT REINFORCEMENTS.
IT'S GOOD TO SEE YOU.
YOU, TOO.
YOU THINKING US THREE SHOULD MAKE A RUN FOR IT?
I DON'T KNOW, RIVAINI...
BETTER THAN WAITING ON THE QUNARI.
UNLESS YOU'D RATHER A FATE BASED ON WHAT THE *HOLY QUN* SAYS ABOUT THE COLOR OF YOUR PISS?
POINT TAKEN.
MAKE SURE ALISTAIR GETS OUT.
YOU UNDERSTAND?
WHERE ARE *YOU* GOING?
TO FIND MY CREW.
THEY CAN STAY OR DIE FIGHTING, BUT THEY DESERVE THE CHOICE.

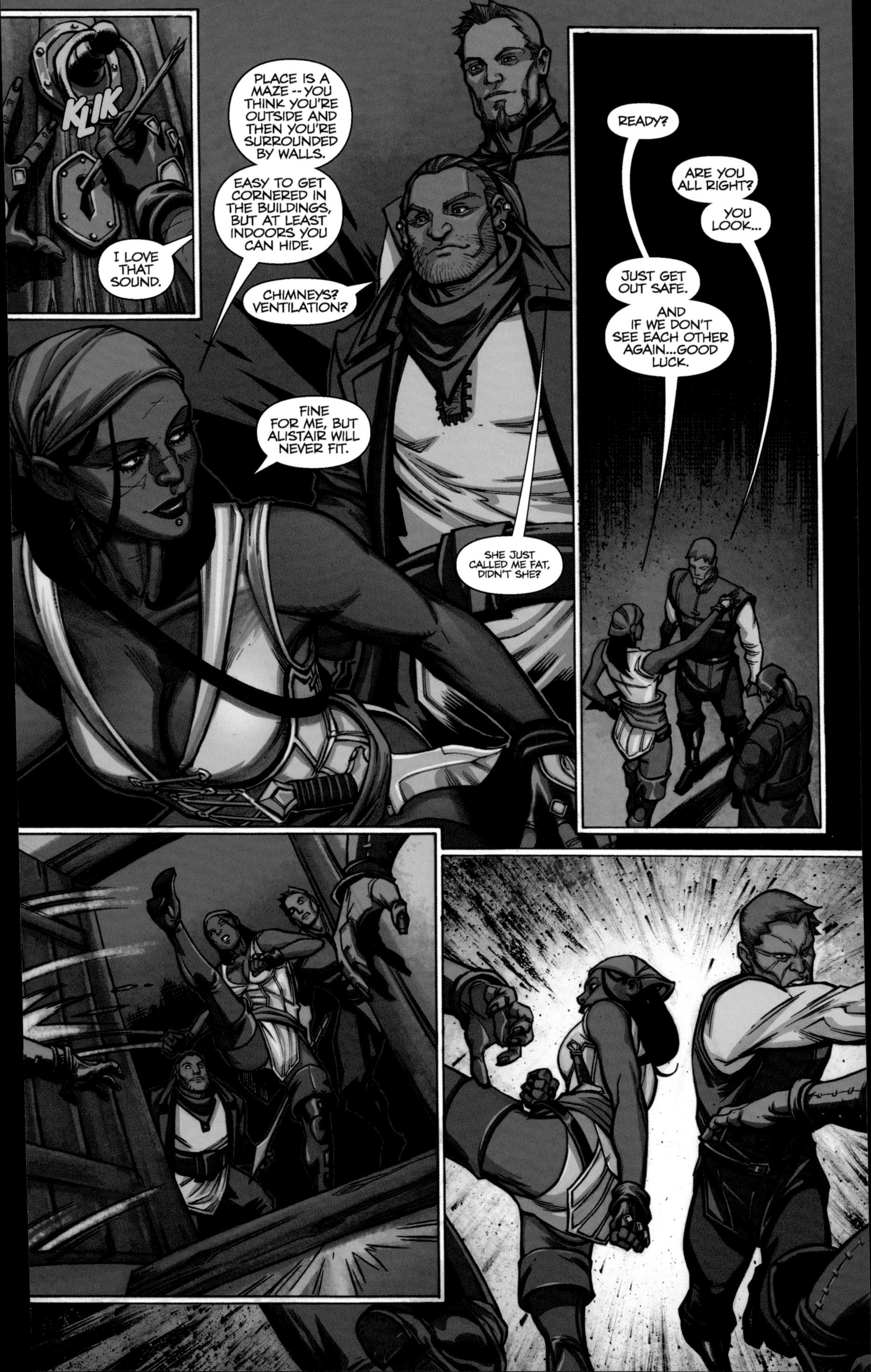
KLIK
I LOVE THAT SOUND.
PLACE IS A MAZE -- YOU THINK YOU'RE OUTSIDE AND THEN YOU'RE SURROUNDED BY WALLS.
EASY TO GET CORNERED IN THE BUILDINGS, BUT AT LEAST INDOORS YOU CAN HIDE.
CHIMNEYS? VENTILATION?
FINE FOR ME, BUT ALISTAIR WILL NEVER FIT.
SHE JUST CALLED ME FAT, DIDN'T SHE?
READY?
ARE YOU ALL RIGHT?
YOU LOOK...
JUST GET OUT SAFE.
AND IF WE DON'T SEE EACH OTHER AGAIN...GOOD LUCK.

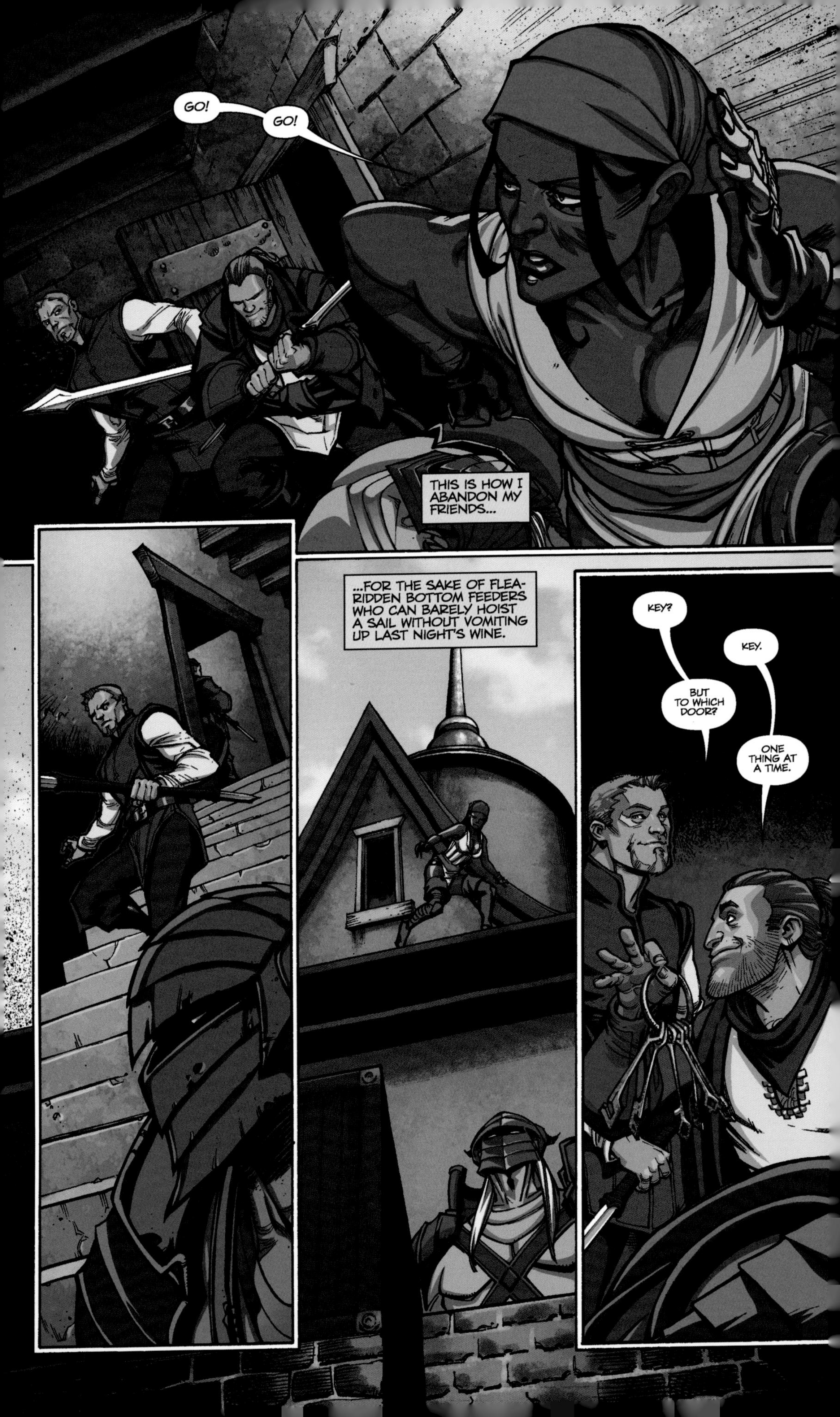
GO!
GO!
THIS IS HOW I ABANDON MY FRIENDS...
...FOR THE SAKE OF FLEA-RIDDEN BOTTOM FEEDERS WHO CAN BARELY HOIST A SAIL WITHOUT VOMITING UP LAST NIGHT'S WINE.
KEY?
KEY.
BUT TO WHICH DOOR?
ONE THING AT A TIME.

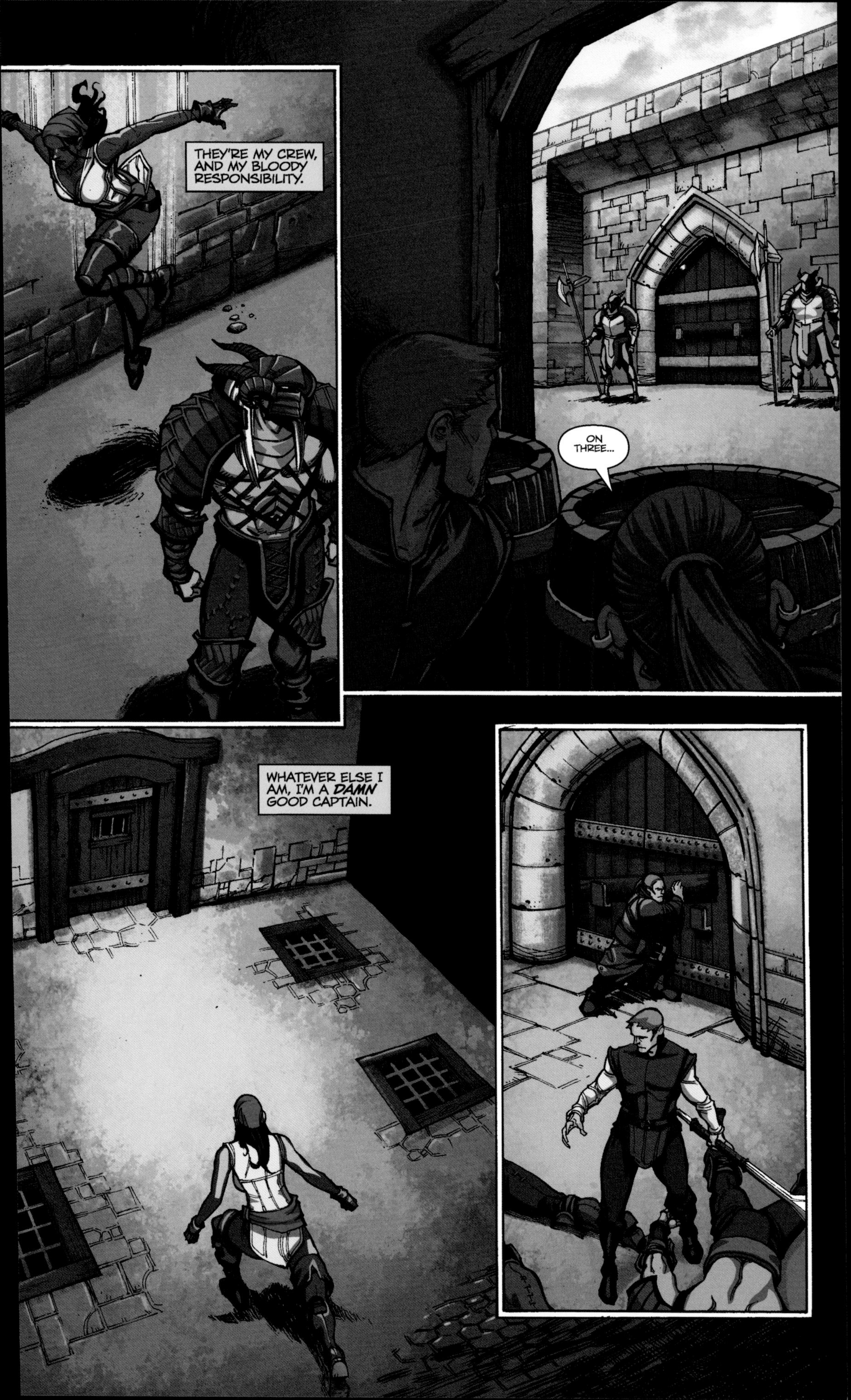
THEY'RE MY CREW, AND MY BLOODY RESPONSIBILITY.
ON THREE...
WHATEVER ELSE I AM, I'M A DAMN GOOD CAPTAIN.

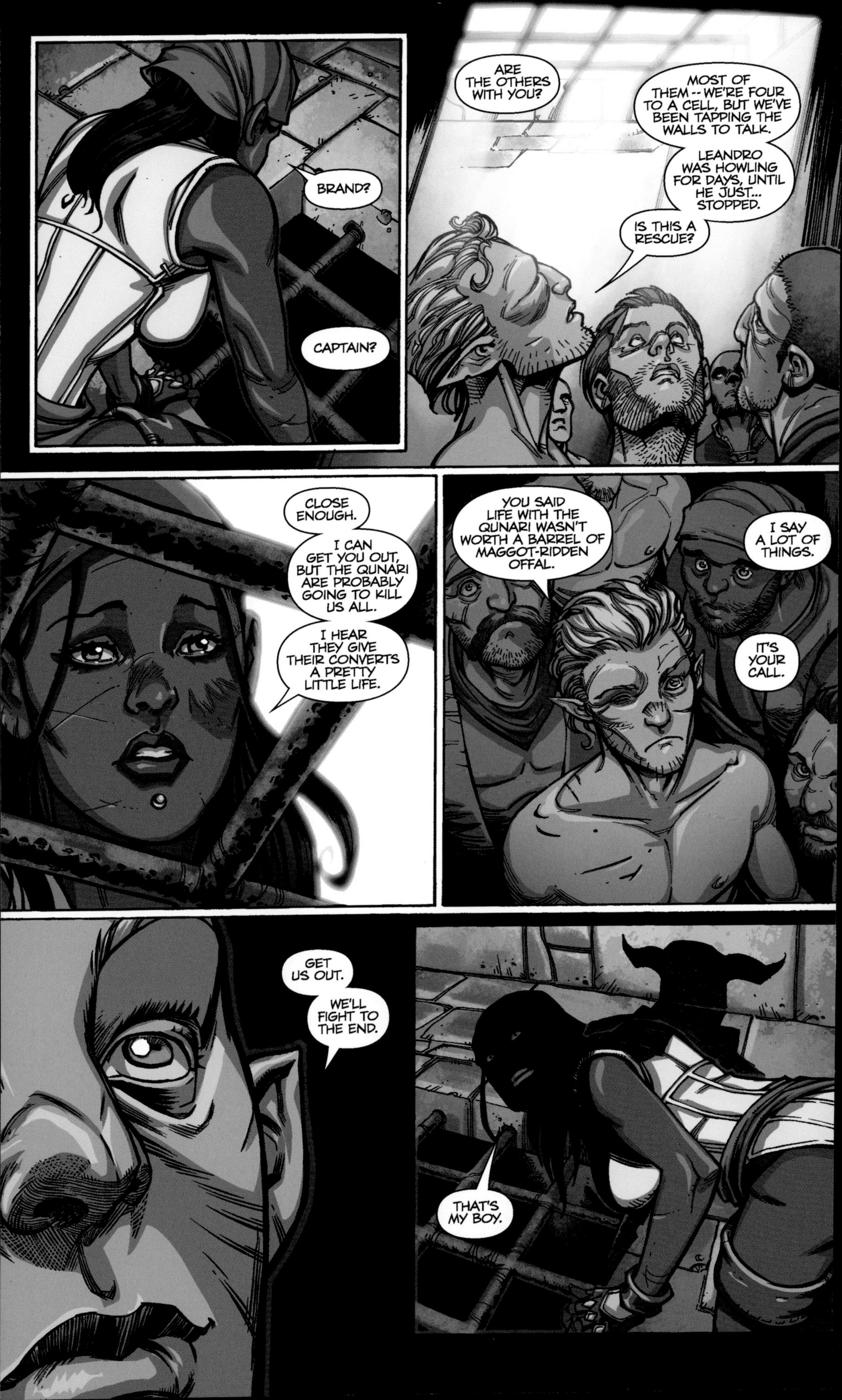
BRAND?
CAPTAIN?
ARE THE OTHERS WITH YOU?
MOST OF THEM -- WE'RE FOUR TO A CELL, BUT WE'VE BEEN TAPPING THE WALLS TO TALK.
LEANDRO WAS HOWLING FOR DAYS, UNTIL HE JUST... STOPPED.
IS THIS A RESCUE?
CLOSE ENOUGH.
I CAN GET YOU OUT, BUT THE QUNARI ARE PROBABLY GOING TO KILL US ALL.
I HEAR THEY GIVE THEIR CONVERTS A PRETTY LITTLE LIFE.
YOU SAID LIFE WITH THE QUNARI WASN'T WORTH A BARREL OF MAGGOT-RIDDEN OFFAL.
I SAY A LOT OF THINGS.
IT'S YOUR CALL.
GET US OUT.
WE'LL FIGHT TO THE END.
THAT'S MY BOY.

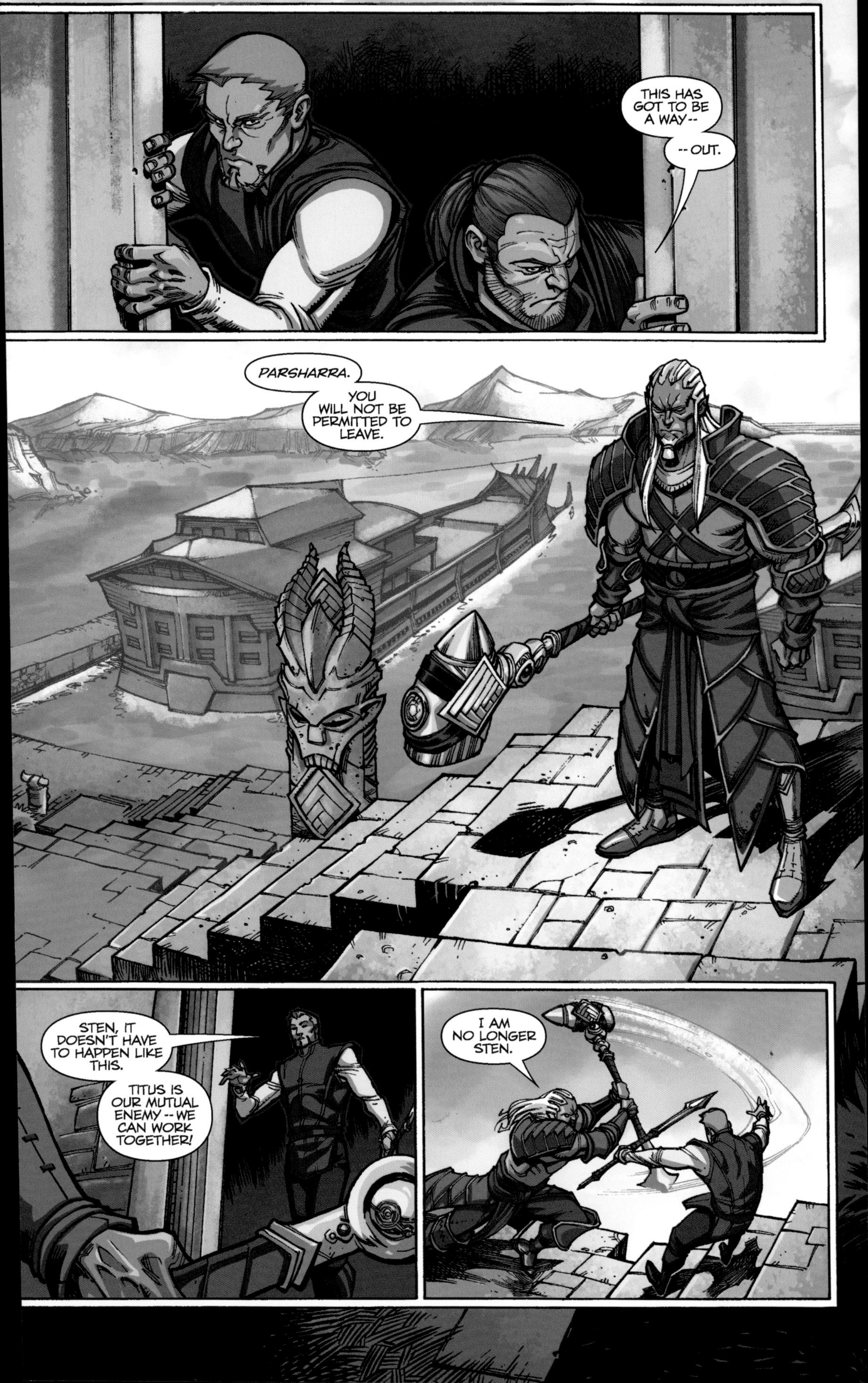
THIS HAS GOT TO BE A WAY--
-- OUT.
PARSHARRA.
YOU WILL NOT BE PERMITTED TO LEAVE.
STEN, IT DOESN'T HAVE TO HAPPEN LIKE THIS.
TITUS IS OUR MUTUAL ENEMY -- WE CAN WORK TOGETHER!
I AM NO LONGER STEN.

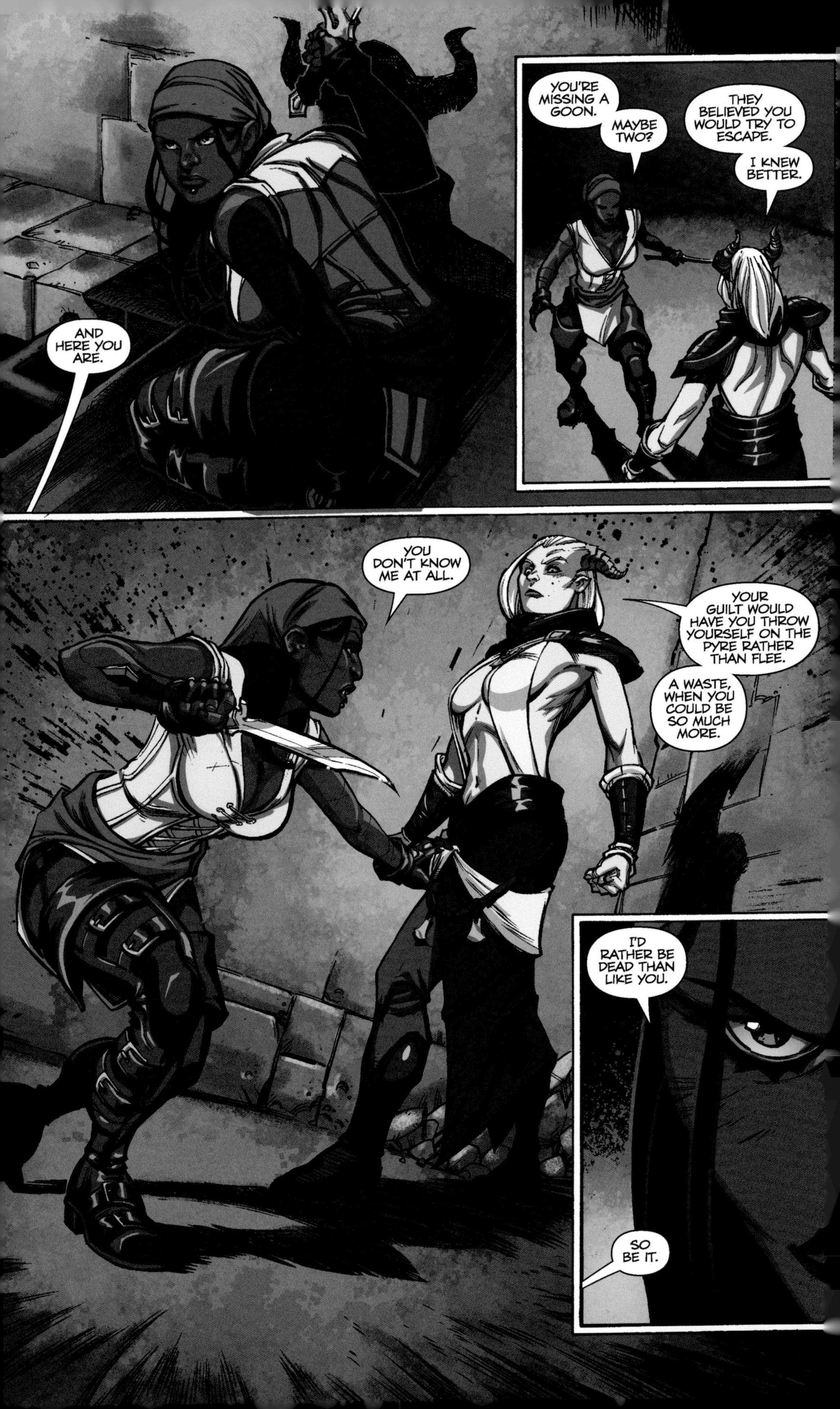
AND HERE YOU ARE.
YOU'RE MISSING A GOON.
MAYBE TWO?
THEY BELIEVED YOU WOULD TRY TO ESCAPE.
I KNEW BETTER.
YOU DON'T KNOW ME AT ALL.
YOUR GUILT WOULD HAVE YOU THROW YOURSELF ON THE PYRE RATHER THAN FLEE.
A WASTE, WHEN YOU COULD BE SO MUCH MORE.
I'D RATHER BE DEAD THAN LIKE YOU.
SO BE IT.

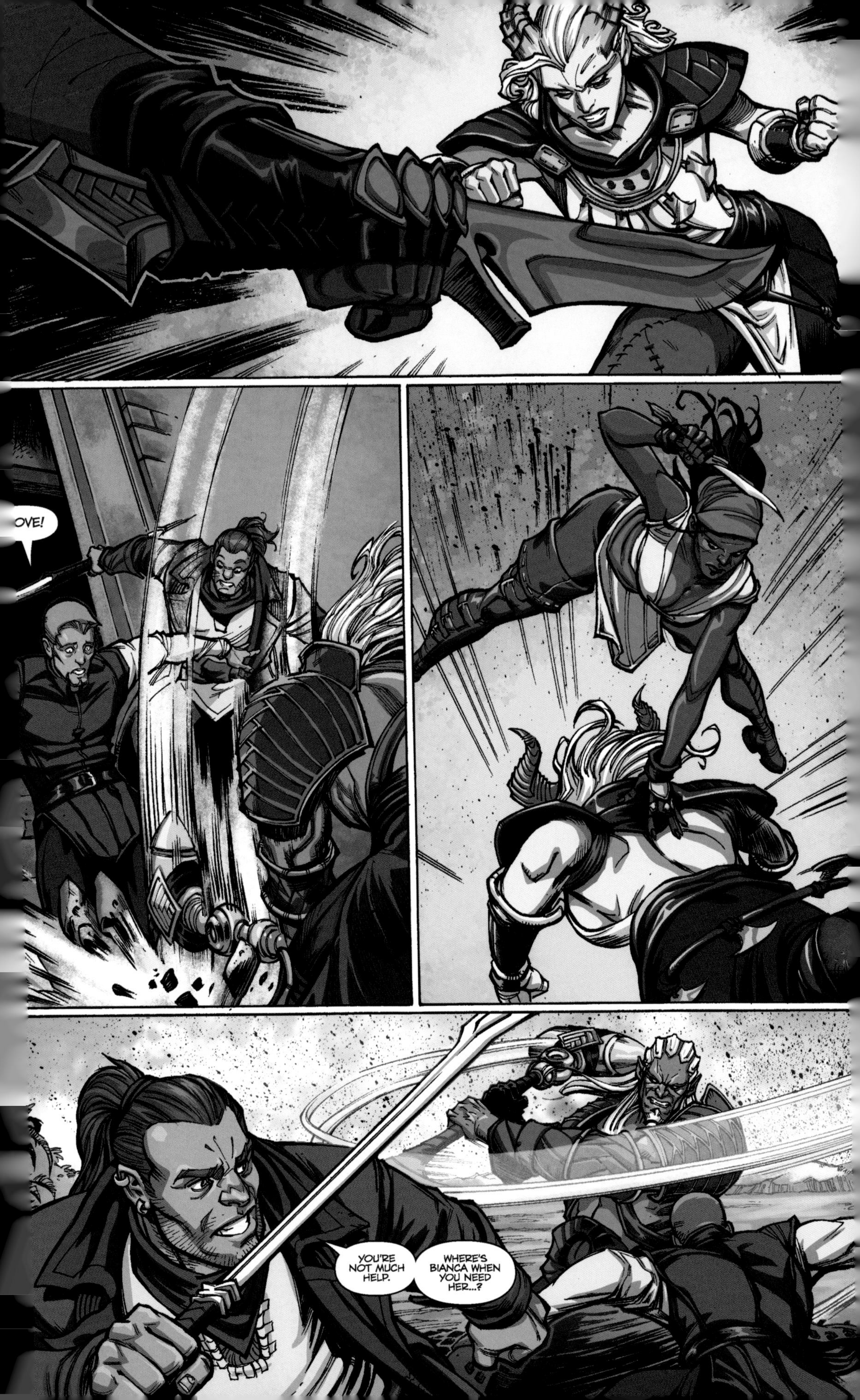
OVE!
YOU'RE NOT MUCH HELP.
WHERE'S BIANCA WHEN YOU NEED HER...?

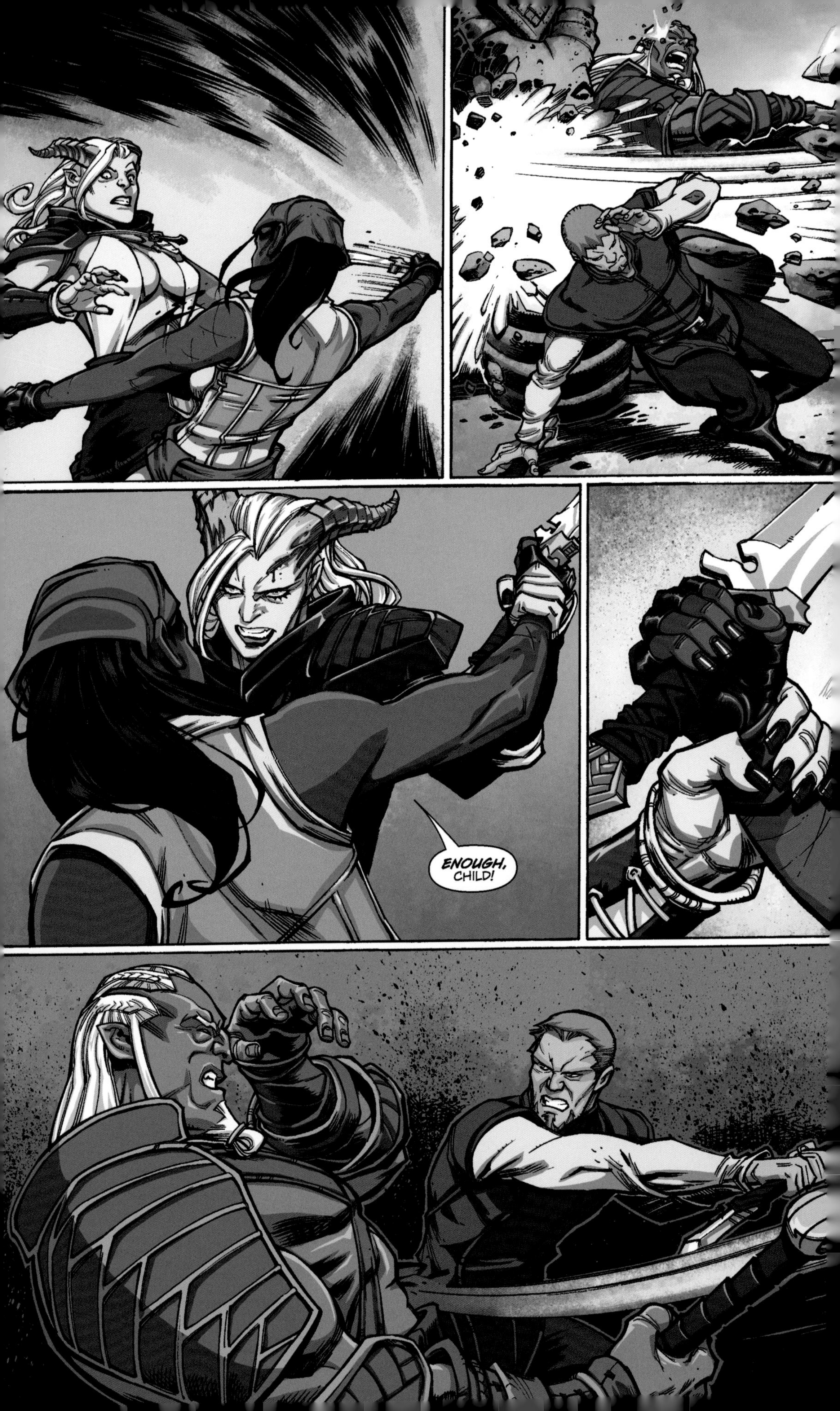
ENOUGH, CHILD!

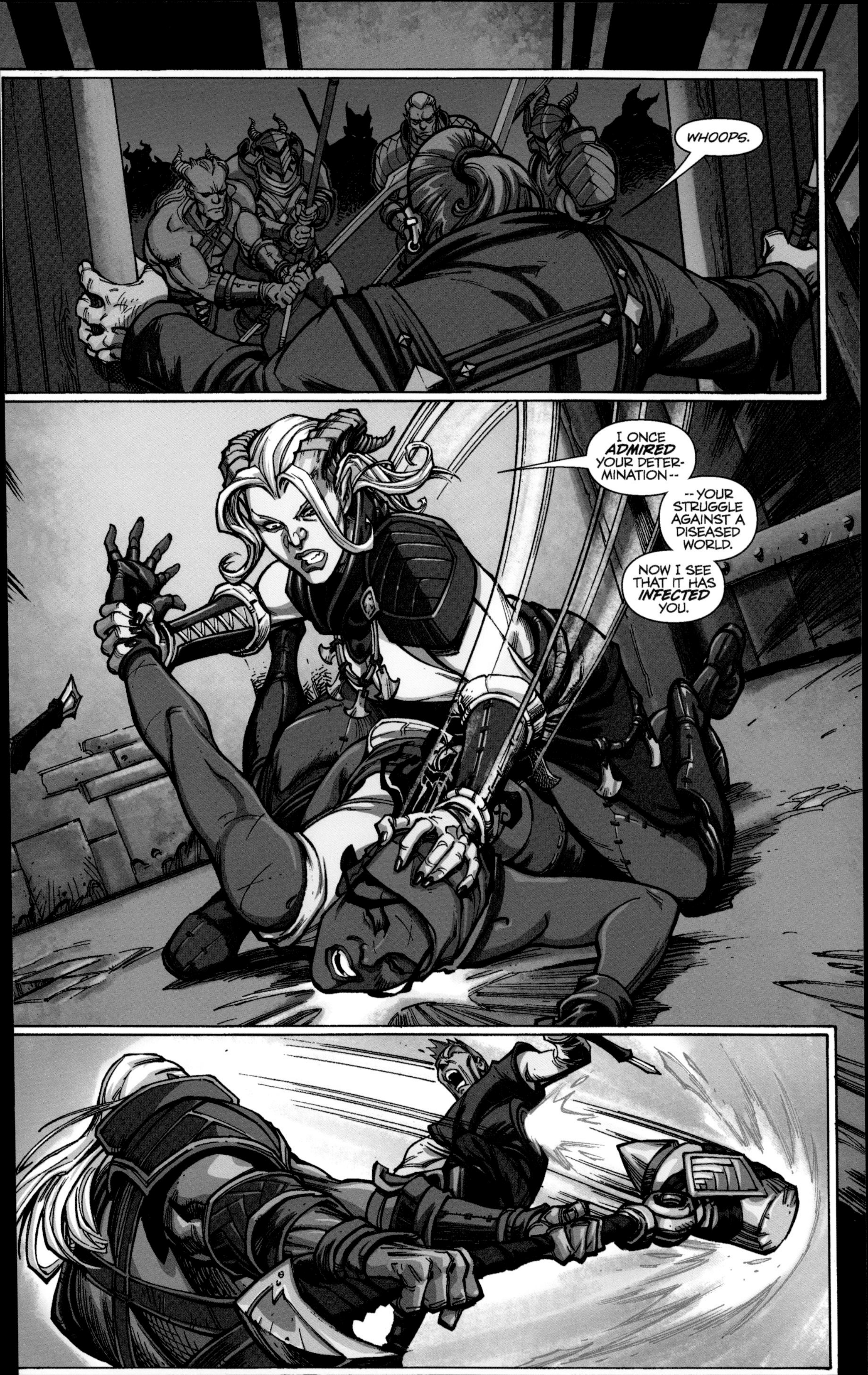
WHOOPS.
I ONCE ADMIRED YOUR DETERMINATION--
--YOUR STRUGGLE AGAINST A DISEASED WORLD.
NOW I SEE THAT IT HAS INFECTED YOU.

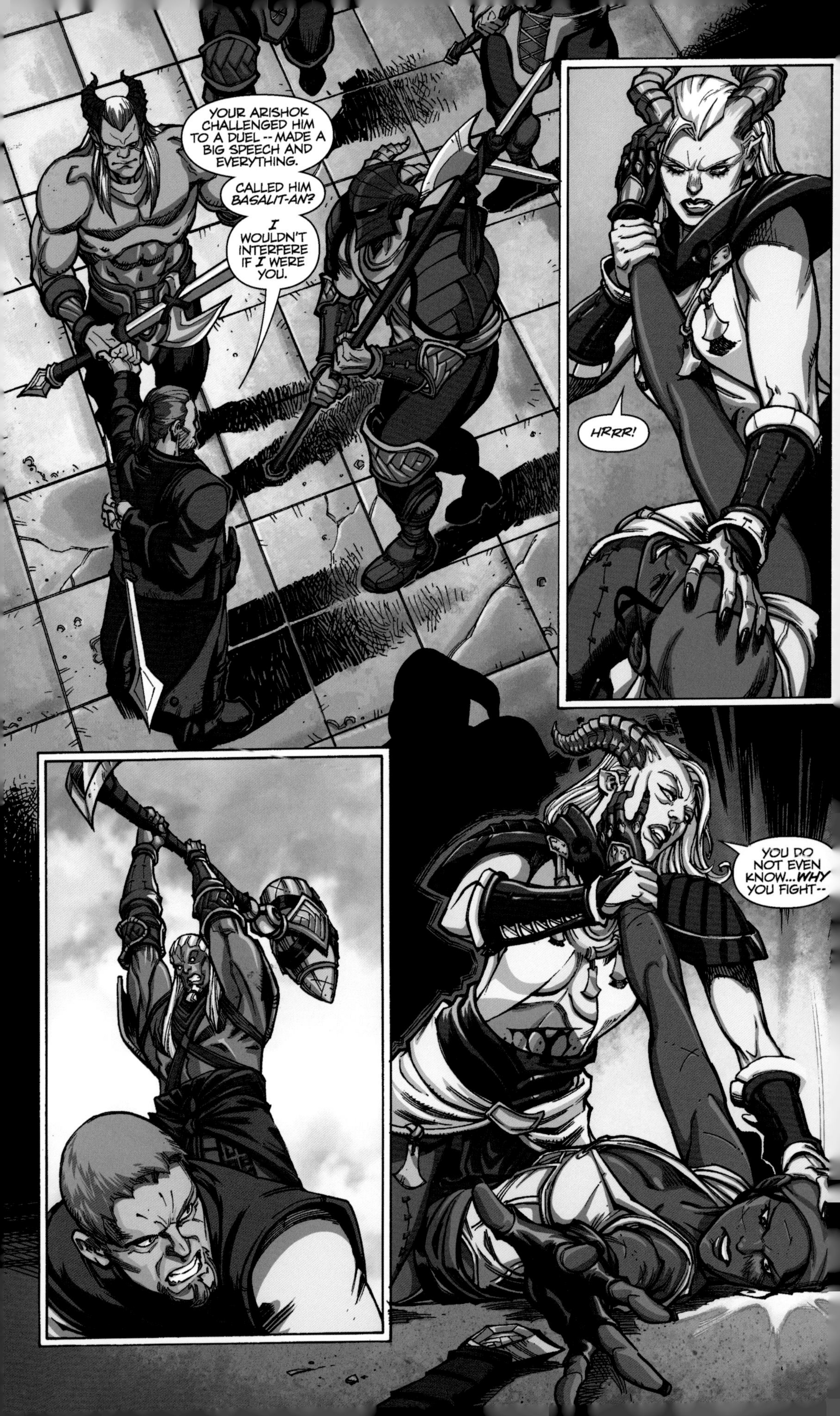
YOUR ARISHOK CHALLENGED HIM TO A DUEL -- MADE A BIG SPEECH AND EVERYTHING.
CALLED HIM *BASALIT-AN*?
I WOULDN'T INTERFERE IF *I* WERE YOU.
HRRR!
YOU DO NOT EVEN KNOW...*WHY* YOU FIGHT--

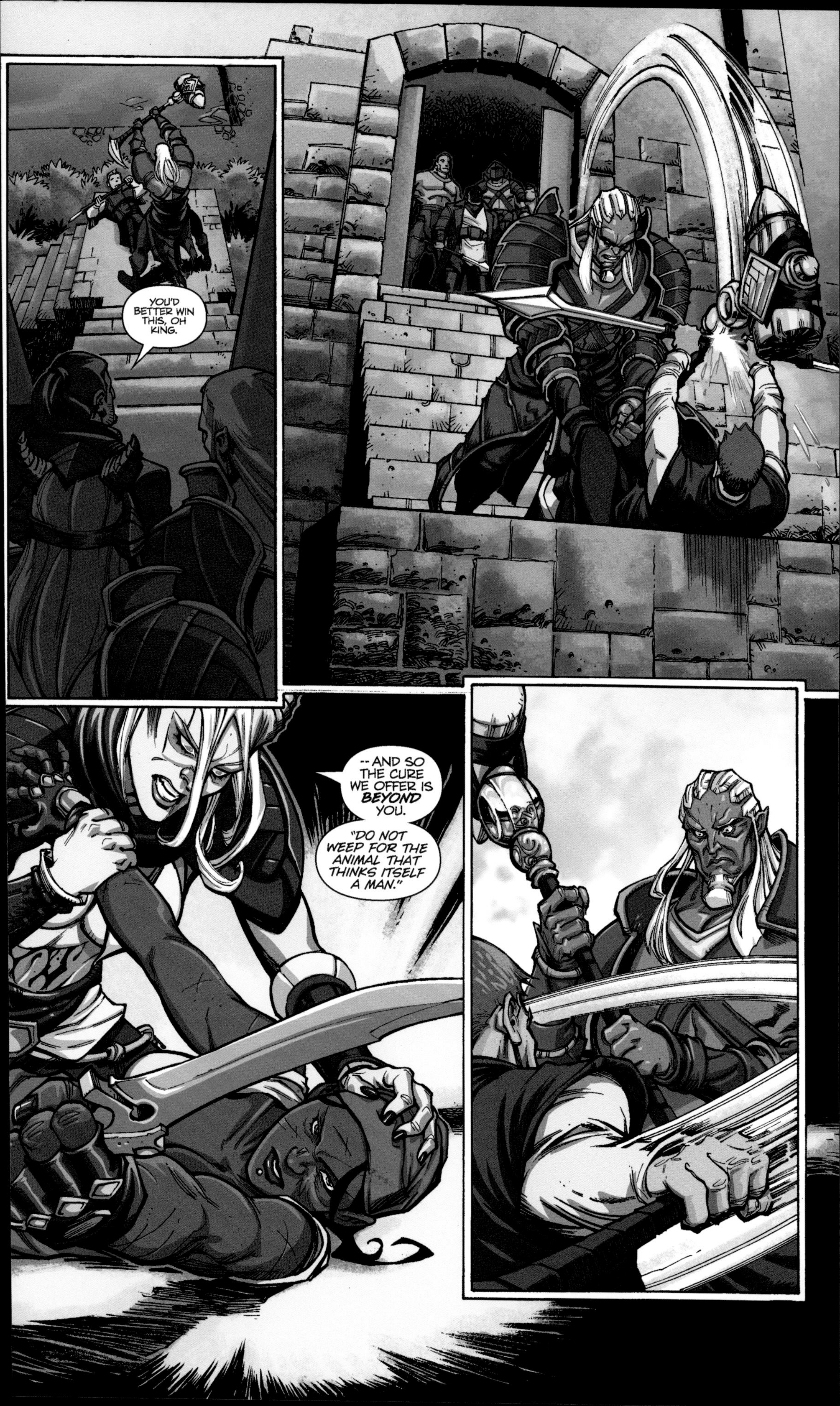
YOU'D BETTER WIN THIS, OH KING.
--AND SO THE CURE WE OFFER IS **BEYOND** YOU.
"DO NOT WEEP FOR THE ANIMAL THAT THINKS ITSELF A MAN."

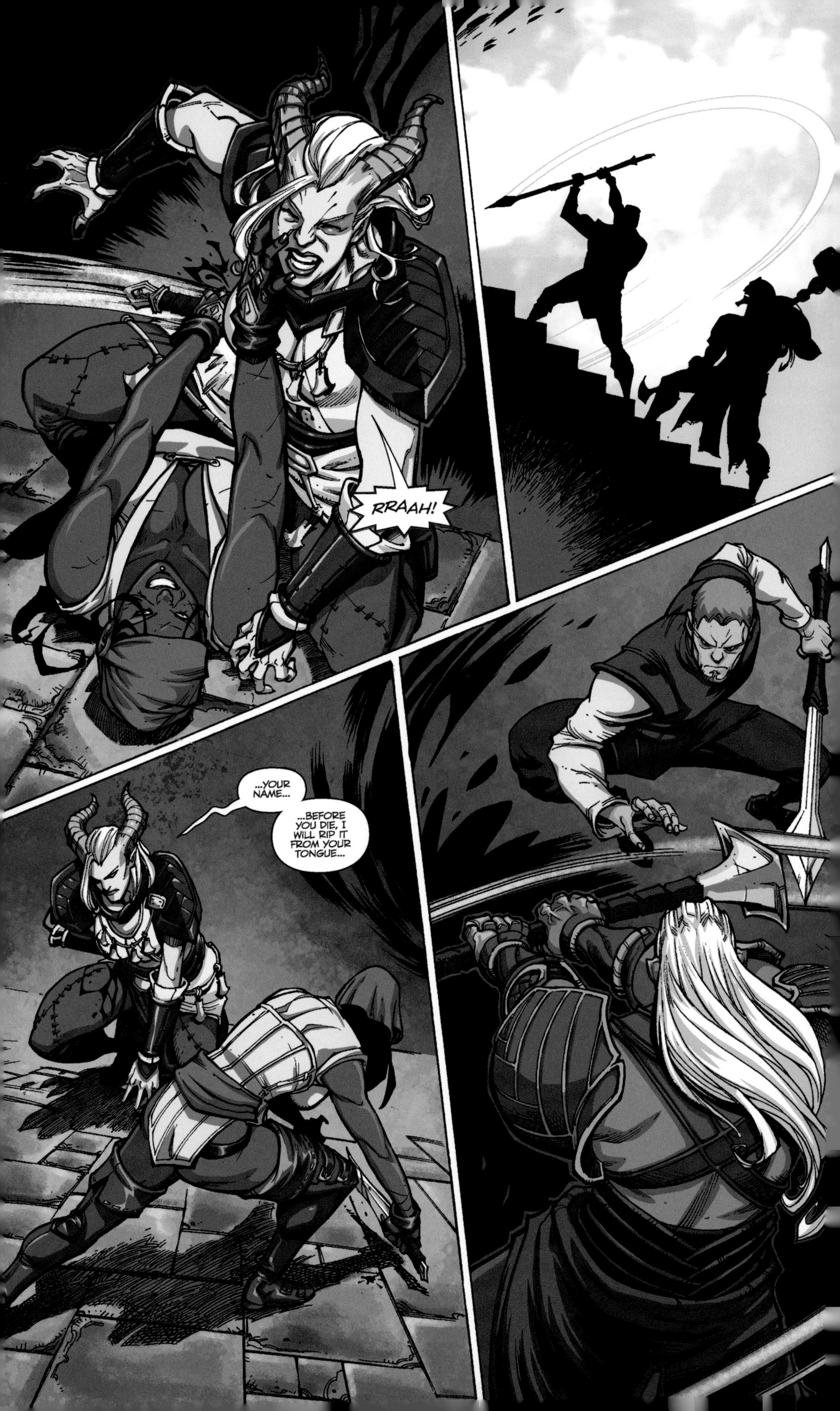
RRAAH!
...YOUR NAME...
...BEFORE YOU DIE, I WILL RIP IT FROM YOUR TONGUE...

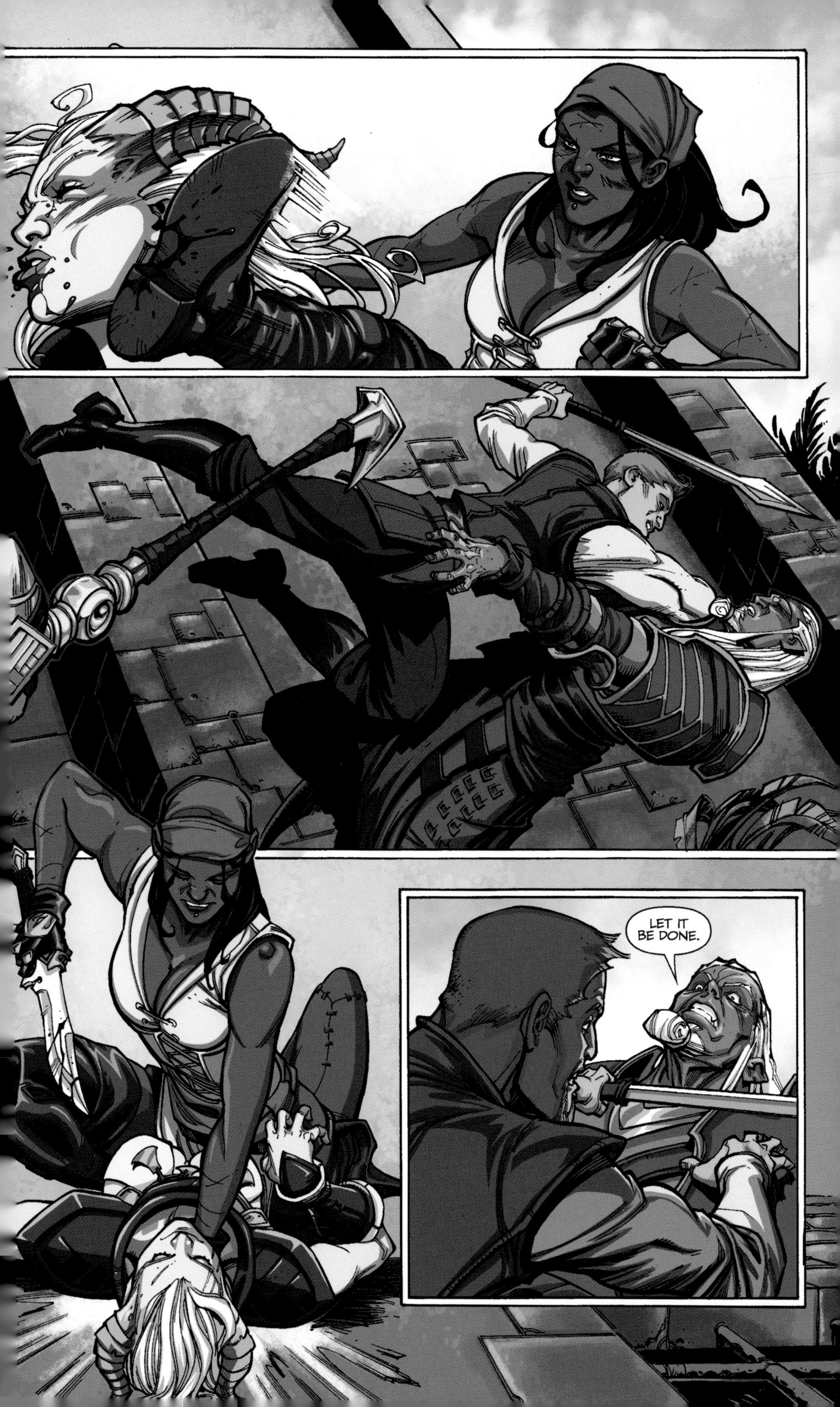
LET IT BE DONE.

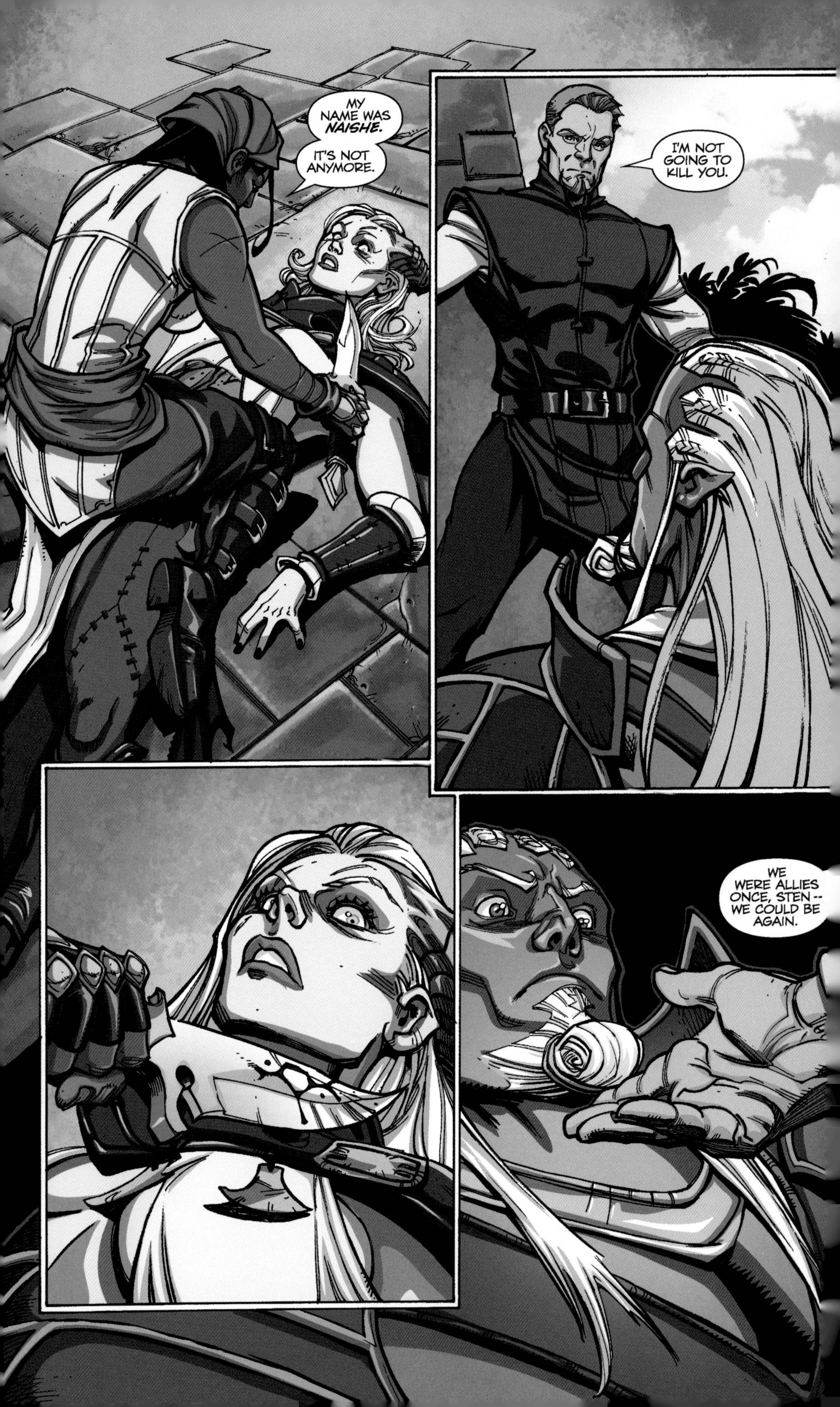
MY NAME WAS NAISHE.
IT'S NOT ANYMORE.
I'M NOT GOING TO KILL YOU.
WE WERE ALLIES ONCE, STEN -- WE COULD BE AGAIN.

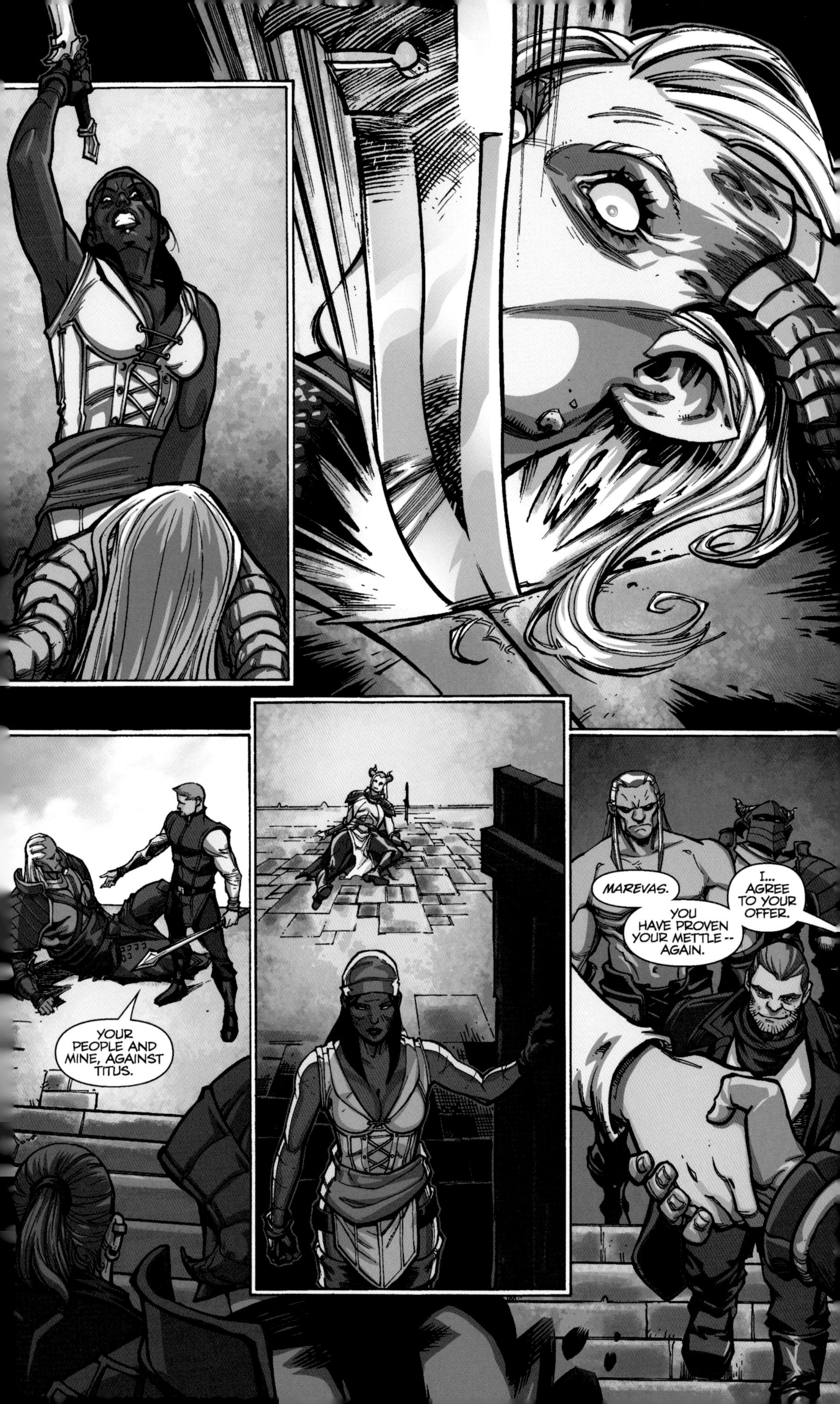
YOUR PEOPLE AND MINE, AGAINST TITUS.
MAREVAS.
YOU HAVE PROVEN YOUR METTLE -- AGAIN.
I... AGREE TO YOUR OFFER.

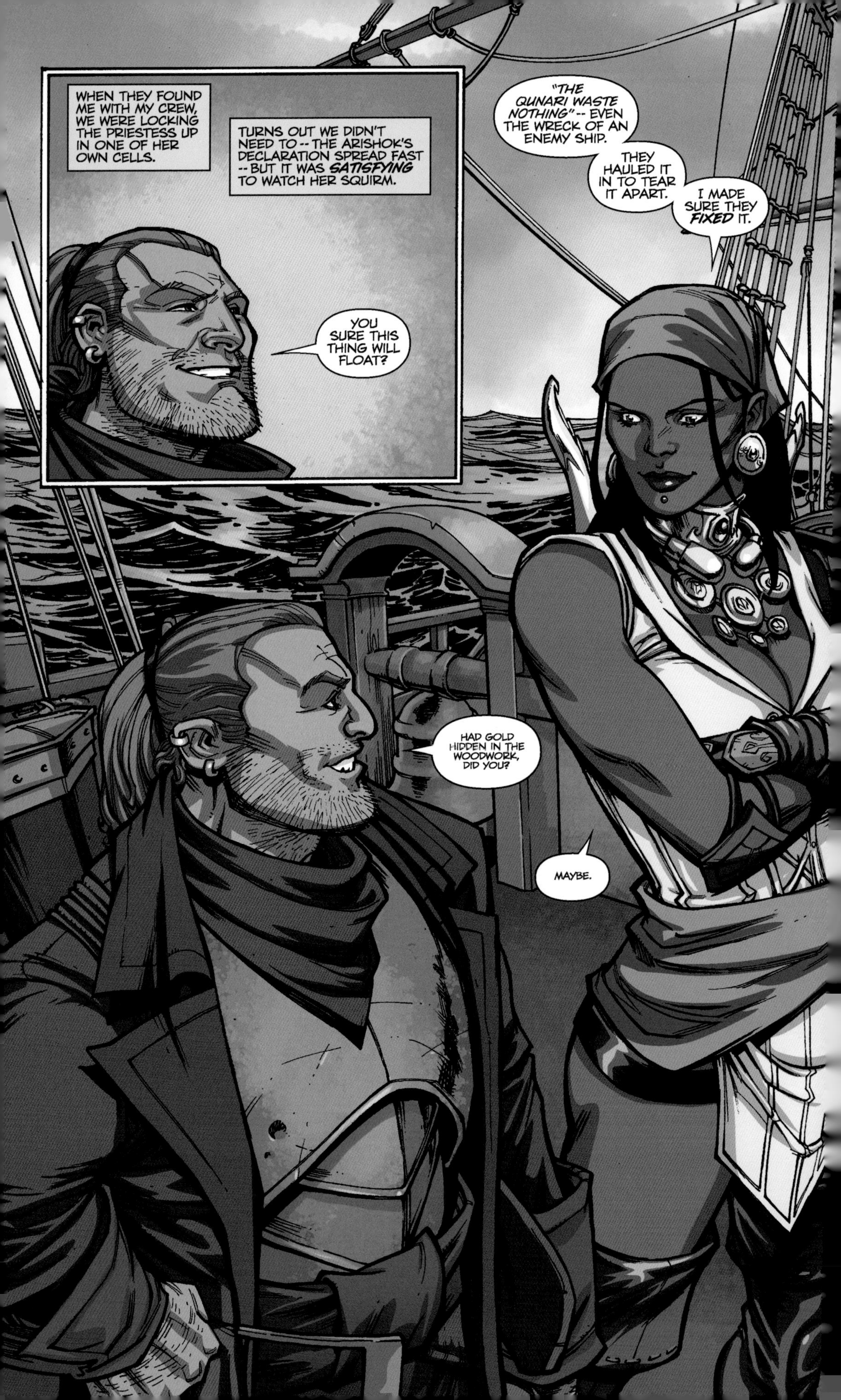
WHEN THEY FOUND ME WITH MY CREW, WE WERE LOCKING THE PRIESTESS UP IN ONE OF HER OWN CELLS.
TURNS OUT WE DIDN'T NEED TO -- THE ARISHOK'S DECLARATION SPREAD FAST -- BUT IT WAS SATISFYING TO WATCH HER SQUIRM.
YOU SURE THIS THING WILL FLOAT?
"THE QUNARI WASTE NOTHING" -- EVEN THE WRECK OF AN ENEMY SHIP.
THEY HAULED IT IN TO TEAR IT APART.
I MADE SURE THEY FIXED IT.
HAD GOLD HIDDEN IN THE WOODWORK, DID YOU?
MAYBE.

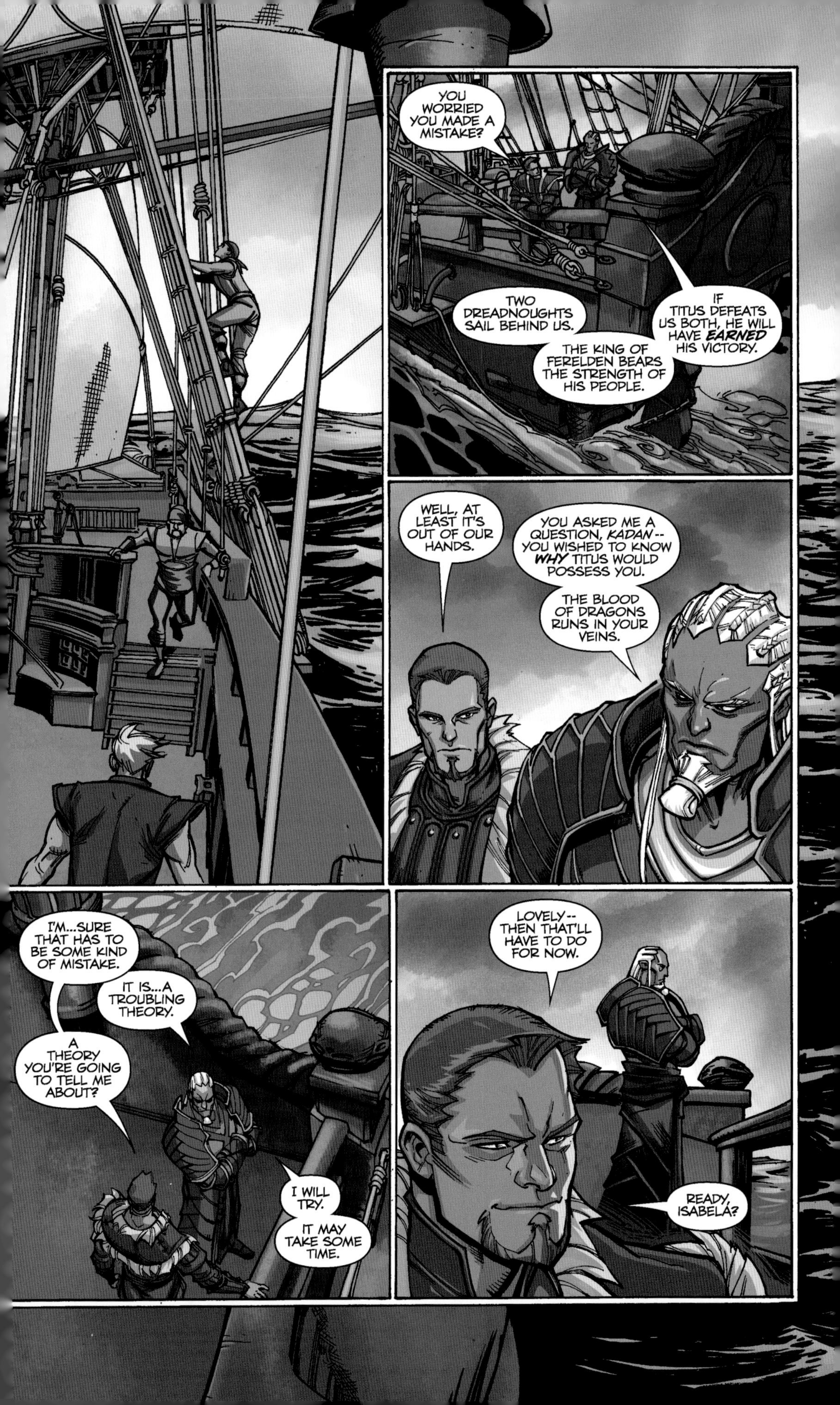
YOU WORRIED YOU MADE A MISTAKE?
TWO DREADNOUGHTS SAIL BEHIND US.
THE KING OF FERELDEN BEARS THE STRENGTH OF HIS PEOPLE.
IF TITUS DEFEATS US BOTH, HE WILL HAVE EARNED HIS VICTORY.
WELL, AT LEAST IT'S OUT OF OUR HANDS.
YOU ASKED ME A QUESTION, KADAN-- YOU WISHED TO KNOW WHY TITUS WOULD POSSESS YOU.
THE BLOOD OF DRAGONS RUNS IN YOUR VEINS.
I'M...SURE THAT HAS TO BE SOME KIND OF MISTAKE.
IT IS...A TROUBLING THEORY.
A THEORY YOU'RE GOING TO TELL ME ABOUT?
I WILL TRY.
IT MAY TAKE SOME TIME.
LOVELY-- THEN THAT'LL HAVE TO DO FOR NOW.
READY, ISABELA?

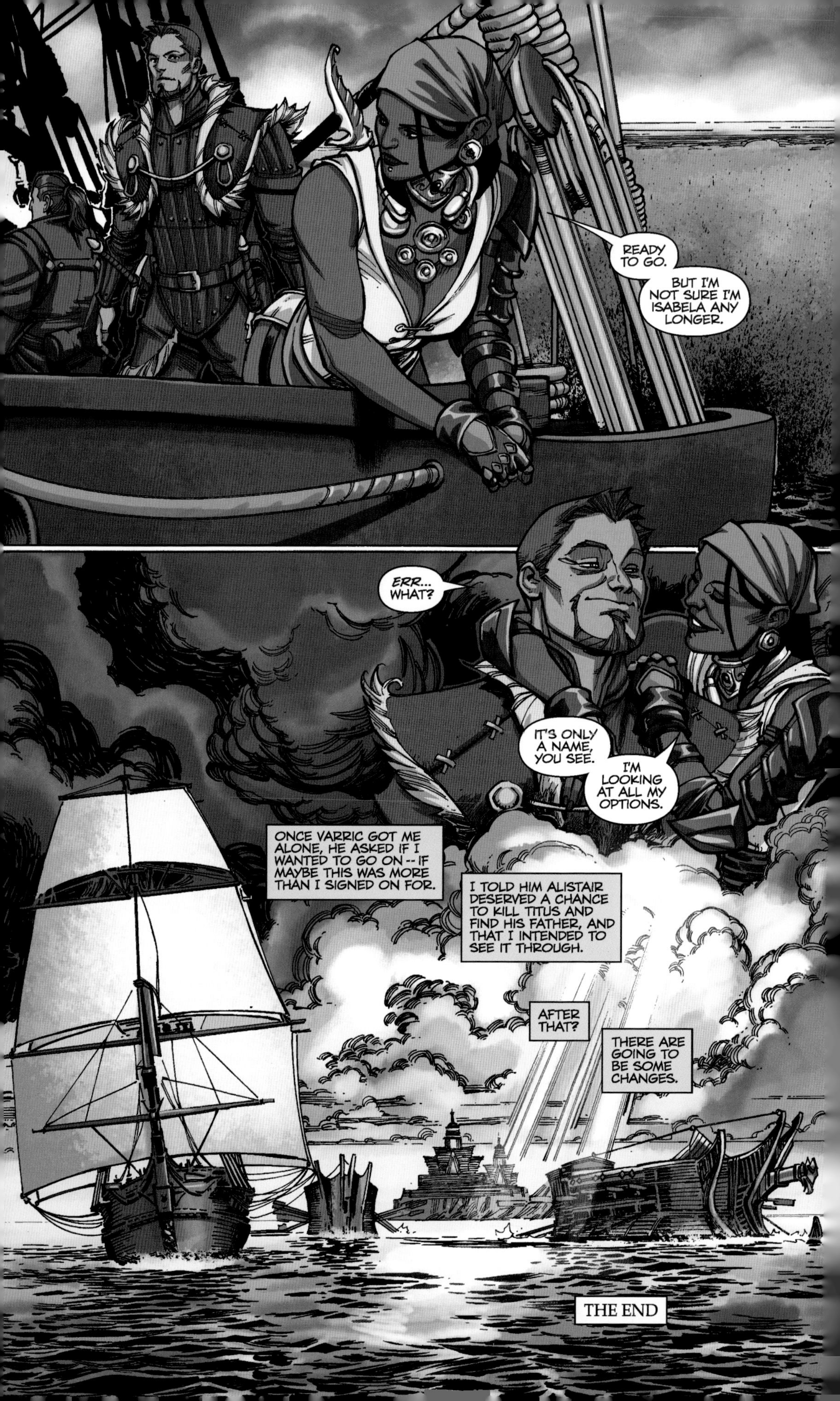
READY TO GO.
BUT I'M NOT SURE I'M ISABELA ANY LONGER.
ERR... WHAT?
IT'S ONLY A NAME, YOU SEE.
I'M LOOKING AT ALL MY OPTIONS.
ONCE VARRIC GOT ME ALONE, HE ASKED IF I WANTED TO GO ON -- IF MAYBE THIS WAS MORE THAN I SIGNED ON FOR.
I TOLD HIM ALISTAIR DESERVED A CHANCE TO KILL TITUS AND FIND HIS FATHER, AND THAT I INTENDED TO SEE IT THROUGH.
AFTER THAT?
THERE ARE GOING TO BE SOME CHANGES.
THE END